CONVERSATION
with...

Q&A with

ALFRED MOISAN

In aid of

FareShare
fighting hunger,
tackling food waste

FareShare registered Charity number 1100051

Book design by NunoRibeiroDesign.com

CONTENTS

WINEMAKERS / VINEYARD OWNERS

SOMMELIERS / MIXOLOGISTS / BAR OWNERS / WINE MERCHANTS

FOOD & DRINKS EXPERTS / JOURNALISTS / AUTHORS

INTRODUCTION BY
ALFRED MOISAN

Hello, my name is Alfred and I am 12 years old. When I am older, I would love to be a chef.

I have written this book during lockdown because I wanted to combine my passion for cooking with raising money for charity so I thought it would be the perfect idea to interview some of the best people in the world who work in the food and drinks sector.

I would like to thank everybody who has contributed to the book. They were very generous with their time when I am sure that they had a lot to worry about with their work. The answers are fascinating and will hopefully inspire a lot of readers.

I also have a special thank you for Stephen Harris (head chef at the Sportsman in the UK) for helping me last year: when I was preparing for a cooking competition (Kent Young Cooks), Stephen and his colleague Theresa gave me advice on presentation for my dish (you can find the recipe in the appendix).

For every sale we make, 100% of profit goes to *FareShare*, the largest charity tackling hunger and food waste in the UK.

Welcome to *In Conversation With* and thank you for supporting *FareShare*!

In this book, there are mentions of wine and other alcoholic drinks.
If you drink, always drink responsibly!

Note from Alfred's parents: We would also like to make it clear that, though Alfred holds a budding chef's interest in the pairing of food and wine, he is sticking to the non-alcoholic components of the dishes for the time being.

FOREWORD BY
WILLIAM DREW,
DIRECTOR OF CONTENT, *THE WORLD'S 50 BEST RESTAURANTS*

FROM KENT TO THE WORLD

I have never met Alfred Moisan and nor, I hazard, have the vast majority of contributors to *In Conversation With...* And yet this remarkable 12-year-old schoolboy has successfully corralled an array of stellar chefs, winemakers, sommeliers and food writers to his cause from all corners of the globe. How so? I think it's because Alfred's original idea, his enthusiasm, his desire to help others and his sheer gumption in pushing ahead with this project against the odds appealed to something in all of us.

Alfred and I both hail from Kent, the far south-eastern country of England known as the Garden of England for its abundance of fresh fruit and produce. We share not only a county, but a fascination with the world of gastronomy, its blend of art and science, alchemy and business, individuality and teamwork. I'm told the author was inspired in part by *The World's 50 Best Restaurants*. I would suggest that we—the 50 Best organisation and the establishments that form part of the ranking—can be inspired by Alfred's achievements, now and no doubt in the future. As an aspiring chef, perhaps one day he will lead a restaurant challenging the very best in the world?

This book captures the spirit of positivity that has been so evident within the hospitality community even when it has been under intense pressure over the pandemic period. The resulting interviews are fun, insightful and forward-lookin—all qualities we remain in dire need of—with all profits going to help fund meals for disadvantaged families via *FareShare*.

So, bravo and three cheers: first, to Alfred and his father, Jerome, whose patient assistance is not to be underestimated. Second, to all the contributors to this book—from Ferran Adrià himself to Kent's own Stephen Harris; Argentinian bar maestro Tato Giovannoni to Australian sommelier Jane Lopes—for giving their time, wisdom and support. Third, to all of you who have purchased a copy: we hope you enjoy being part of this project as much as we have and are inspired to harness the power of hospitality as a force for good.

Let's all raise a glass of Chateau d'Yquem to that.

ABOUT
FARESHARE

FareShare is the UK's biggest charity fighting hunger and food waste—diverting surplus food, which would otherwise go to waste, to people at risk of hunger through our network of frontline charities and community groups nationwide.

MESSAGE FROM *LINDSAY BOSWELL,*
CHIEF EXECUTIVE, *FARESHARE*

A huge thank you to the incredible Alfred for supporting *FareShare*. Funds raised through this book will make a huge difference to our organisation. They will be helping to get good food out to communities, who are facing hunger across the UK.

We whole-heartedly share in Alfred's passion for food. Across our warehouses, *FareShare* delivers an enormous variety of surplus food including fruit, vegetables, dairy, meat, tins and more. This food helps tackle hunger, giving people the opportunity to try new ingredients and cook recipes they might not have been able to afford otherwise.

At *FareShare*, it is our strong belief that everyone should have access to a good meal and the chance to enjoy a healthy nutritious diet. Thanks to Alfred and his wonderful book more people will be able to do just that.

FareShare registered Charity number 1100051

CHEFS

RESTAURANT OWNERS

Ferran Adrià

HEAD CHEF, *ELBULLI*, ROSES, SPAIN

3 MICHELIN STARS AND MULTIPLE WINNER OF THE WORLD'S BEST
RESTAURANT AWARD; NOW PROMOTING THE ELBULLI FOUNDATION

**Do you take a year off to travel the world and discover new foods
and wines? What's your 2-3 country itinerary?**

I have been able to travel to wonderful places with cultures as diverse as Asia and South America. Perhaps now
I would dare to travel to other places not as well-known
as African cuisine such as Tanzania or Angola to be able
to know their customs or products.

Who are the four people you would dream of having dinner with?

I love being around people from other disciplines or artists like Israel Ruiz from MIT, great publicists like Luis
Cuesta or Toni Segarra, Vicente Todoli former director of
Tate Modern or the great architect Frank Ghery. They all
bring different visions that help me learn and see new
perspectives on everything that I can apply to the kitchen.

What was your most memorable food/wine pairing at a restaurant?

One has many left in the memory, but without a doubt
the best moment was the last dinner at elBulli as a restaurant, where the menu was a compilation of its great
dishes with the best wines and the great Bullinianos
as chefs like Jose Andres, Heston Blumenthal, Massimo
Bottura, etc.

**Is there anything that no one knows about you? Or something that
people don't realize?**

I love watching documentaries about animals or history.
I like to learn and take walks on the beach very early.

If you weren't working in the food and wine industry, what profession would you like to have learned?

The footballer I loved when I was little (and who I wanted to be) is Johan Cruyff.

What is your most unusual food/wine combination that you would recommend?

I am very simple, the pleasure can be in eating a good fried egg with a barrel wine.

What is the biggest myth about prestigious wines?

That they have to be expensive, there are wines that are currently made that are very good and you can find them at reasonable prices. Then there are other extraordinary ones that are paid as such, the extraordinary must always be paid.

How do you relax outside of work?

The truth is that we could say that I do not work, I have made a profession a way of life. I no longer have a restaurant and now I run a foundation that has become my life. Outside of this, I go to restaurants to eat, I visit places to learn about their culture, I enjoy local produce, etc.

What advice would you give your 21 year old self?

I would tell young people to take life with passion, to be passionate about what they do, and to seek to understand what they do, to question the status quo, to take nothing for granted, not to settle for dogmas, not to stay in pragmatism and strive to get things done.

What surprising wine do you have in your cellar?

It's not a wine, it's a champagne: a Dom Perignon 2006 vintage.

Stephen Harris

HEAD CHEF, *THE SPORTSMAN*, SEASALTER, UK
MICHELIN STAR AND 5 TIMES WINNER OF THE BEST
RESTAURANT IN THE UK AWARD

If you were to die and come back as an ingredient, what would it be?

I would like to come back as a langoustine because I like the big pincers or a lobster because they can live for over a hundred years.

You take one year off to go travelling around the world to discover new cuisines? What is your itinerary of 2–3 countries?

I would love to go to Mexico to eat and learn the street food. I would also love to go to learn about Thai food by going on a cooking course 'up the river'. Back, in the 1990s all the Aussie chefs talked about going 'up the river' in Thailand. It was part of their education in food. I know very little about Cambodian and Vietnamese food but while I was in the area I would love to learn more. The whole region of South East Asia is very exciting.

What is the best advice you've been given that has helped you along the way?

Keep your knives sharp! It makes life so much easier.

Who are the four people you'd dream about having dinner with?

John Lennon, Robert Johnson, Marc Chagall and my partner Emma. She would be jealous if I didn't ask her along! I like to hear how artists and musicians work and I would bring some guitars for them to play.

What was your most memorable meal as a customer in another restaurant than your own?

A meal at Chez Nico back in the 1990s. It was the meal which got me into cooking to a high standard. Everything was perfect-bright and vivid—on the plate and in the mouth

Is there something nobody knows about you/your restaurant? Or something people don't realise?

My chefs have been with me for a long time: Dan, the head chef, has been with me for 21 years and Russell, the sous chef, for about 13 years and others.

If you were not a chef/restaurateur, what profession would you like to have learnt?

I was a teacher and a financial consultant so I had the chance to try other things so that when I became a chef, I knew it was what I wanted to do. Many chefs end up doing the job by accident but I chose it.

You are given (unlimited) funds to acquire a vineyard of your choice? Which one would you buy?

Romanee Conti in Burgundy. I love the grape Pinot Noir and this is the best example of it anywhere in the world. If I was clever, I would find somewhere a bit further north that grew great pinot noir as the changing climate means everything will have to shift north.

If you could have one superpower, what would it be?

I would love to fly. You can get anywhere really easily and avoid the traffic. I often look at birds and think how lucky they are.

What is your most unusual food/wine combination that you would recommend?

Salmon with Syrah. I once cooked some salmon with a champagne and wild strawberry sauce and we drank Crozes Hermitage with it. It was a stunning combination.

What is the biggest myth about famous chefs/restaurants?

Restaurants are like theatre-they are performances every night. In reality many are tough places to work: the back of house is very different to the front, where the customers eat. It is getting better but chefs need to learn how to treat their staff properly.

Do you have a funny anecdote about a meal/dish that went wrong?

Never let your mistakes leave the kitchen. I am always playing with ideas because you never know what will work. I once thought that a dish of poached pears, soda bread, and blue cheese would be delicious but it was revolting.

How do you relax outside of cooking?

I play guitar and like reading and watching films with my son, Stanley.

What advice would you have for your 21-year-old self?

I wish I knew that if you want to achieve anything you have to work hard. I was lucky that I was good at sport and music but I didn't work hard because they came easily. By the time I became a chef at 33, I had learned that if I wanted to succeed, I had to work very hard.

How would you like to be remembered?

If I am remembered, that would be good enough.

Virgilio Martinez

HEAD CHEF, *CENTRAL*, LIMA, PERU
3 TIMES WINNER OF THE BEST RESTAURANT IN LATIN AMERICA

If you were to die and come back as an ingredient, what would it be?

As a potato. Some potatoes in the Andes are wild and they stay in the soil for many years just in peace

You take one year off to go travelling around the world to discover new cuisines? What is your itinerary of 2-3 countries?

I would go to the Amazon of any other country that is not Peru (I want to discover different jungles); it is special to get to see this amount of wild nature. Then I would fly to Oaxaca to eat. Then to Japan, any hidden place, any mystic place where I get to see something very different to what I normally see and taste food too.

What is the best advice you've been given that has helped you along the way?

Not to compete with people; compete with who I was yesterday. Do not compare yourself to others, try to be a better person. Be authentic. Do not give excuses or try to be another person

Who are the four people you'd dream about having dinner with?

My grand-parents; I miss those beautiful stories about the family. I lost them when I was still a little kid so I remember very little but what I got from them is beautiful

What was your most memorable meal as a customer in another restaurant than your own?

It was at Asador Etxebarri (Spanish restaurant in Atxondo, Basque Country), in 2015. Just pure quality of ingredients, the taste of fire and the short, honest conversation I got at the end with the chef made a magical finish.

Is there something nobody knows about you/your restaurant? Or something people don't realise?

I enjoy talking to people a lot but as a cook, it is getting difficult to get the time. Some people think I am so focused in the kitchen and that's true but I am trying to figure out how to get more time in the future to see people with whom I have lost track and good friends I made during my career.

If you were not a chef/restaurateur, what profession would you like to have learnt?

An architect, I like design; I love to see the process of building things .

You are given (unlimited) funds to acquire a vineyard of your choice? Which one would you buy?

It would be in France, the obvious Champagne region and its quality, tradition, luxury

If you could have one superpower, what would it be?

Fly

What is your most unusual food/wine combination that you would recommend?

Amazonian fish with warmed wines, I mean natural wines with the addition of ingredients from the Amazon like crazy fruits and cane

What is the biggest myth about famous chefs/restaurants?

That we are celebrities or that we live as if everything is under control, surrounded by people that make things for us, because it is the opposite!

Do you have a funny anecdote about a meal/dish that went wrong?

Yeah the fish with a salted crust: I was serving in the dining room, breaking the salt from the fish that was in the dish and the thing was that there was only salt—I forgot to put the fish! It was so embarrassing. But it was all sorted out with a big apology and a smile.

How do you relax outside of cooking?

Skateboarding

What advice would you have for your 21-year-old self?

Be disciplined, and be careful who you hang out with. These are the best times to absorb emotions and knowledge before actually being a chef so don't waste that time.

How would you like to be remembered?

By my son, as a great man; somebody that he could name once in a while with anecdotes.

10 QUICK-FIRE QUESTIONS

Eric Ripert

HEAD CHEF,
LE BERNARDIN,
NEW YORK, USA

3 MICHELIN STARS

ARTIST OR ENGINEER?
ARTIST

STARTER OR DESSERT?
BOTH

APERITIF OR DIGESTIF?
APERITIF

BOOK, TV OR TABLET?
BOOK

SPRING, SUMMER, AUTUMN OR WINTER?
SPRING

SEASIDE, MOUNTAIN, CITY OR COUNTRYSIDE?
SEASIDE

STILL OR SPARKLING?
STILL

FICTION OR NON-FICTION?
FICTION

MUSIC OR SILENCE?
SILENCE

SIGHT, SOUND, SMELL, TASTE OR TOUCH?
SIGHT

Julien Royer

CHEF-OWNER, *ODETTE*, SINGAPORE

3 MICHELIN STARS

If you were to die and come back as an ingredient, what would it be?

Flour. It's the foundation of many delicious foods like bread for instance, which is one of my favourites.

You take one year off to go travelling around the world to discover new cuisines? What is your itinerary of 2–3 countries?

I wish I had the time! I love travelling and feel very fortunate to have the opportunity to discover the world as part of my job—experiencing and learning from various cultures, discovering new traditions, tasting unfamiliar ingredients, meeting fantastic people along the way no matter where I am. I believe you should let go of expectations and let life surprise you.

I'd love to return to Japan to learn more about their fascinating culinary history—whether a snack off the street or fine-dining—it is consistently executed at the highest quality with respectable discipline. I really want to go to Hokkaido, we work with a lot of produce from there so it would be fascinating to visit the source. New Zealand is another country that's high on my list. It's such a beautiful place, full of nature and fresh air.

What is the best advice you've been given that has helped you along the way?

I always remember this sentence from Paul Bocuse: 'When you think you've arrived, then you're going to fail,' and this is exactly what it is—a constant learning exercise. We need to question ourselves daily and ask what we can do better than yesterday and what we can do to improve every day.

It's never a winning game, it's not a sprint. It's a marathon.

Who are the four people you'd dream about having dinner with?

Currently, I would say my family back home. I haven't been able to visit them in over a year due to the pandemic. Many of my fondest memories involve spending time with loved ones over a heart-warming meal—in those moments, I forget all my worries. That's the beauty of it.

What was your most memorable meal as a customer in another restaurant than your own?

Elkano in Getaria, Spain. The experience was simply phenomenal—the food is so honest and humble, yet outstanding in quality and flavour. They've kept to the same techniques and modest recipes since opening in the 1960s. Such an unforgettable experience.

What is the biggest myth about famous chefs/restaurants?

We love to sing in the kitchen! There are moments of high pressure but it doesn't mean we don't ever have fun. I want Odette to be a place where my team looks forward to coming to work each day. Music is so important in setting the mood, and everyone takes turns to decide on the playlist for the day.

If you were not a chef/restaurateur, what profession would you like to have learnt?

A rally driver. Speed and intensity are two things I'm drawn to in any profession, and you definitely find that working in a kitchen too although in a different manner.

You are given (unlimited) funds to acquire a vineyard of your choice? Which one would you buy?

Mas de Daumas Gassac. The estate is absolutely beautiful and the wine is superb.

If you could have one superpower, what would it be?

Invisibility.

What is your most unusual food/wine combination that you would recommend?

Cauliflower and coconut. Both ingredients have a nutty and slightly sweet flavour so they complement each other very well.

Do you have a funny anecdote about a meal/dish that went wrong?

There was once we left a white asparagus velouté to chill in the freezer, it ended up freezing into a granita but it was delicious. That's the beauty of food, sometimes unexpected outcomes can lead to surprising discoveries.

How do you relax outside of cooking?

I like to start the day by having breakfast with my wife, Agnes. We always make time to do so even in the mornings before work. On my days off, I usually get together with friends to play tennis, drink wine or watch football matches especially when Paris Saint-Germain (PSG) are playing.

What advice would you have for your 21-year-old self?

Stay true to yourself and what you believe in. Be humble, never stop learning from the people around you—your peers, partners, and fellow creators. It is important to continuously broaden your world views and expose yourself to differing perspectives.

How would you like to be remembered?

As someone who was joyful and full of life, who brought good, positive energy to those around him.

Manish Mehrotra

CORPORATE CHEF, *INDIAN ACCENT*, NEW DELHI/NEW YORK
No. 1 CHEF IN INDIA, THE ECONOMIC TIMES, 2018

If you were to die and come back as an ingredient, what would it be?

Coconut as it is hard from outside but soft from inside. It can be used in various forms. The complete tree is used for several things.

You take one year off to go travelling around the world to discover new cuisines? What is your itinerary of 2–3 countries?

I'd travel to Mexico, Japan and South Africa to eat, learn and explore various ingredients and cuisines.

What is the best advice you've been given that has helped you along the way?

Hard work never fails and the foundation should be solid.

Who are the four people you'd dream about having dinner with?

Amitabh Bachchan, Julia Roberts, Mahatma Gandhi, Queen Elizabeth II. These are the people I admire and am a huge fan of. Would love to curate a menu for them someday!

What was your most memorable meal as a customer in another restaurant than your own?

The Mushroom tasting Menu at Mathias Dahlgren in Stockholm is one of the best I have ever had.

Is there something nobody knows about you/your restaurant? Or something people don't realise?

Not really.

If you were not a chef/restaurateur, what profession would you like to have learnt?

I'd be a film star. I acted as a child actor in a film.

You are given (unlimited) funds to acquire a vineyard of your choice? Which one would you buy?

Cloudy Bay in New Zealand! I love that wine and it goes perfectly with Indian food

If you could have one superpower, what would it be?

Healing with food!

What is your most unusual food/wine combination that you would recommend?

Champagne with Indian Chaat

What is the biggest myth about famous chefs/restaurants?

That they cook for their family every day!

How do you relax outside of cooking?

Watching movies.

What advice would you have for your 21-year-old self?

Take care of my health and stay fitter.

How would you like to be remembered?

As a good chef, who highlighted the Indian Cuisine on a global platform.

Jessica Craig

PASTRY CHEF, *SANDBAR ON HUDSON*, NEW YORK
PREVIOUSLY AT L'ARTUSI AND ALMOND RESTAURANTS

If you were to die and come back as an ingredient, what would it be?

I think I would come back as salt, Kosher Salt specifically. I use it and sprinkle it on everything.

You take one year off to go travelling around the world to discover new cuisines? What is your itinerary of 2–3 countries?

I would go to Australia because I've been before and absolutely loved it. I also follow a few Australian pastry chefs and I would love to try their desserts and pastries. The cuisine there is so interesting because there are so many ingredients that are unique to Australia that aren't available in the USA that I would love to explore.

It's really tough just choosing three countries! I'd also go to China and I think the last place I would choose on my world travel is Morocco.

What is the best advice you've been given that has helped you along the way?

The best advice I have ever been given is to never settle. Always seeking the best in every situation has helped me advance my career and to find the best situations possible for my life.

Who are the four people you'd dream about having dinner with?

Michelle Obama because I think she's simply fabulous. She is smart, stylish, and uses her influence to create positive good in the world.

Another person is Janelle Monae. I love her music. I also met her briefly before she became as famous as she is now and she is so nice and kind. She is open about all aspects of who she is as well as speak up on social issues that are important.

Jessica Harris is an African American Food Historian. I'd love to have dinner with her to simply tap into her knowledge. She also has had significant time spent with people such as Maya Angelou and James Baldwin. I can only imagine a fascinating conversation with her.

Andy Cohen, I think would be the fun party guy I'd invite to dinner. He has access to so many celebrities and has had an amazing career in relation to reality TV. His priorities have clearly changed since he's had his son but I would still imagine a great time.

What was your most memorable meal as a customer in another restaurant than your own?

I think the most memorable meal I've had as a customer at a restaurant is at Loring Place in NYC. They have a very seasonal menu. You can tell the thought and care that is put into every aspect of the diner's dinner experience.

Is there something nobody knows about you/your restaurant? Or something people don't realise?

I don't think most people who don't work in the restaurant industry understand how much thought and planning goes into their whole experience. Recipes are tested and tasted multiple times, sourcing great ingredients, adding special touches to make the experience exceptional, etc. You hope that those who dine at your establishment notice all the care you pour into it but sometimes when it seems effortless, a lot goes unnoticed.

If you were not a chef/restaurateur, what profession would you like to have learnt?

I would have gotten into music. I took piano for a short while as a kid. A part of me wishes I didn't give it up. I have thought of picking it up again as a hobby.

You are given (unlimited) funds to acquire a vineyard of your choice? Which one would you buy ?

I would acquire Wolffer vineyard. The grounds are gorgeous. It's so beautiful. They had a limited-edition dessert wine a few years back that I fell in love with. They offer a non-alcoholic cider that is so delicious too.

If you could have one superpower, what would it be?

I would love to have the superpower of teleportation. That would save so much on travel time. I love to travel but the act of travelling can be exhausting.

What is your most unusual food/wine combination that you would recommend?

I'm not sure if this is the most unusual but I love a red Lambrusco with almost anything fatty. Especially with a well-made roasted or seared duck. Yum!

What is the biggest myth about famous chefs/restaurants?

I think the biggest myth about chefs in particular is that they need to be fat in order to be a good one. Can we put that to rest? The size of someone's physical appearance has no bearing on their cooking abilities.

Do you have a funny anecdote about a meal/dish that went wrong?

I worked at a restaurant a long time ago where I used to

be the first person in the kitchen. I made a few big batches of ice cream base to help get us ahead as we were in the busy season at the moment. The pastry chef came in and started to chat with me and while I had my back turned, I saw her frown slightly and then heard a big thud. Ice cream base was everywhere. I wanted to cry and thankfully she was very understanding. I can laugh about it now but then I couldn't have been more upset.

How do you relax outside of cooking?

I like to go for nature walks. I also like to listen to music. I have a playlist that I call 'Mood Boosted' specifically if I need to lift my mood. I also like to dance. Sometimes I also do a full body stretch or meditate.

What advice would you have for your 21-year-old self?

Take a year off and live abroad for a while. I think that's my only regret about my career. I wish I'd spent time in Paris or Australia both places I've had the privilege of visiting but would love to spend significantly more time learning about the food and culture. I was so focused on getting my career going I not regret taking a bit of down time to explore the world around me.

How would you like to be remembered?

I would like to be remembered as a pastry chef who is talented at her craft but is a genuinely good human who does her best to help those she loves and her community at large.

David Higgs

HEAD CHEF, *MARBLE AND SAINT*, JOHANNESBURG, SOUTH AFRICA

MARBLE RASAA BEST RESTAURANT IN SOUTH AFRICA, 2018

If you were to die and come back as an ingredient, what would it be?

Lemons and limes. Because they are so versatile and just add life to everything, not only the juice but also the zest.

You take one year off to go travelling around the world to discover new cuisines? What is your itinerary of 2–3 countries?

I would definitely like to spend a few months travelling in Japan. It's a country with such a rich history of food products and culture, and for me that would be the ultimate. I've also never been to South America—a country such as Peru with such close ties to the East has always intrigued me.

What is the best advice you've been given that has helped you along the way?

Be patient, persevere and don't think you can get to the top straight away. Young chefs battle to prove themselves and they need to stick it out. One needs to be fairly aggressive in their career: fight for positions and don't worry about upsetting a few people along the way—that's how it is. This is an incredibly competitive industry, and you have to have a go-getter's attitude.

Who are the four people you'd dream about having dinner with?

My Father. I never had a chance to cook for him. He ignited my passion for cooking, and I would have loved to have had the opportunity to cook for him and have a long conversation about things that I have questions about.

Scarlett Johannson. She's lovely.

Lance Armstrong. I am a massive cycling enthusiast, and I have so many questions. I have a no-nonsense approach to everything I do, so I would like to sit down with him and have a conversation.

Anthony Bourdain. To talk stories of kitchens and what went on... things that trouble us—get us down. It would be interesting, someone who understands this and can express themselves.

What was your most memorable meal as a customer in another restaurant than your own?

Although I have had many incredible meals in Italy, I ate a dish at the Spice Temple in Australia that has always stuck with me. It was a dish of steamed aubergine and spicy pork mince—lots of coriander and garlic that you mix through. I was on my way to the airport to fly back to South Africa and only had a little gap, so I sat in the bar and had one or two dishes. I ordered the aubergine dish three times. It might have been one too many, but it was delicious—the simplicity of it—incredible flavours never to be forgotten.

Is there something nobody knows about you/your restaurant? Or something people don't realise?

Many people who see me at the restaurants think that I am a calm, collected person. In fact, I have massive anxiety. I stress an incredible amount so I am not as calm as it may seem.

If you were not a chef/restaurateur, what profession would you like to have learnt?

I think I would have still been in a creative industry. Art has always been a massive love for me—photography and architecture in particular.

You are given (unlimited) funds to acquire a vineyard of your choice? Which one would you buy?

Imagine that! I think it would either be a vineyard in Stellenbosch or one of the old-world vineyards in Tuscany—something like Antinori. I can't think of anything better than being able to ride through Tuscany and then farm there—it would be idyllic.

If you could have one superpower, what would it be?

Not giving a f**k about what people think and say about my food. I take this too personally and this creates stress which feeds my anxiety.

What is your most unusual food/wine combination that you would recommend?

I love the saltiness of anchovies together with a chilled red wine—something that would stand up to them. A lovely Cab would be a great pairing and a little unusual. I also love Riesling paired with curry.

What is the biggest myth about famous chefs/restaurants?

Probably the biggest myth is that they make lots of money.

Do you have a funny anecdote about a meal/dish that went wrong?

In 2004 or 2005, we did an event for Elton John—it was a four-course meal for 440 people at a wine farm in Stellenbosch. After plating the cold starter, we put all the plates on trollies and wheeled them into the back of a refrigerator truck, unfortunately the brakes weren't locked, and two trollies rolled out the back of the truck. This was about half an hour before the start... we lost 140 plates.

How do you relax outside of cooking?

Balance is important, especially for a Chef when you work long hours on your feet and are often under immense pressure. Time out for me often involves my mountain bike—I live for mountain biking and for a number of reasons—exercise, getting outdoors and meeting people. It clears my mind and is a beautiful way to see a country. I've cycled across South Africa, and in a number of European countries and there's nothing quite like discovering places on a bike—by myself.

What advice would you have for your 21-year-old self?

I don't think I would have changed anything in my career—I made the right choices and have had the opportunity to work with great chefs and businessmen who showed me various strengths and ways of promoting your business and self. So, I would probably just tell myself to give myself a bit more time and find more balance. I really did submerge myself into work so didn't get enough out of my 20s as I could have.

How would you like to be remembered?

My career has been successful because when people come to eat at one of my establishments, they know they will get looked after and get a great meal—I've done this consistently over 32 years of my cooking career. I would want people to know that I always gave them the best meal possible, was consistent and someone to be trusted.

Jake Barwood

HEAD CHEF AND FOOD EDUCATOR

TOTTERIDGE ACADEMY (FARESHARE COMMUNITY FOOD MEMBER), UK

If you were to die and come back as an ingredient, what would it be?

A leek. They're humble, tough and have got lots of layers to them!

You take one year off to go travelling around the world to discover new cuisines? What is your itinerary of 2-3 countries?

I've visited a few areas in India and fell in love with the food, especially in the South of the country. I would love to go back and travel some other areas in that vast and beautiful country, and also visit Sri Lanka, and see what delicious food it has to offer!

What is the best advice you've been given that has helped you along the way?

Good manners costs nothing.

Who are the four people you'd dream about having dinner with?

Johnny Cash, Anthony Bourdain, Amy Winehouse, Nye Bevan.

What was your most memorable meal as a customer in another restaurant than your own?

It has to be Le Gavroche. My girlfriend treated me to a meal there for my birthday, I got to chat with Michel Roux Junior and finally got to taste their infamous Soufflé Suissesse!

If you were not a chef/restaurateur, what profession would you like to have learnt?

I have always dreamed of being an explorer or travelling journalist (think Levison Wood). The chance to see some of those remote and extreme parts of the world would be amazing, plus I'm sure I could pick up some good food ideas too.

If you could have one superpower, what would it be?

Octopus tentacles for arms would definitely come in handy when deliveries come in or you've got a few dishes on the go!

Do you have a funny anecdote about a meal/dish that went wrong?

A few years ago, I was catering at a very high-end event during London fashion week. We arrived with our canapes ready to go, only to find out that the event organisers had completely messed up and thought we were supplying the bar (although this was never ever discussed!) They had no wine, no soft drinks and not even any glasses for people to drink out of, so it ended up with a load of media executives running into a Sainsbury's Local near Trafalgar Square to buy up all the wine and plastic cups in the shop!

How do you relax outside of cooking?

Listening to music, exercise and seeing friends.

What advice would you have for your 21-year-old self?

Follow your interests and remember that your career is not always going to be a clear trajectory. Keep doing what you love doing, build good relationships and doors will always open.

How would you like to be remembered?

As the guy who got school kids to eat kimchi!

Greg Malouf

**CHEF/AUTHOR, LEADING EXPERT IN MIDDLE
EASTERN CUISINE, AUSTRALIA/UAE**

ONE OF AUSTRALIA'S MOST INFLUENTIAL AND ADMIRED CHEFS

If you were to die and come back as an ingredient, what would it be?

Yoghurt; it's very versatile! It can be strained and turned into yoghurt cheese. It can be used to tenderize, marinate, it can be made into sauces, desserts, dressings and made into a drink

You take one year off to go travelling around the world to discover new cuisines? What is your itinerary of 2-3 countries?

South America. Brazil, Argentina, Bolivia, Peru and Cuba. I know very little about their cuisines, however I'm a meat lover and also love the fact that a lot of vegetables originated in these regions

What is the best advice you've been given that has helped you along the way?

Restraint! This helped me understand that less is more

Who are the four people you'd dream about having dinner with?

Frank Zappa, Gregory Peck, both my former wives. They have inspired me in some way through my life

What was your most memorable meal as a customer in another restaurant than your own?

Zamponi in Paris circa 1981. It's actually a dish from Modena, Italy made from the front trotter of a pig which is stuffed with a mixture of lean pork meats, belly, back skin, back fat and boiled. It's sliced and sits on braised lentils. The version I had was in a sticky broth. Incredible

Is there something nobody knows about you/your restaurant? Or something people don't realise?

I've had two heart transplants. Not a common thing to share

If you were not a chef/restaurateur, what profession would you like to have learnt?

How to fly a plane! Travel is the major source of information for me

You are given (unlimited) funds to acquire a vineyard of your choice? Which one would you buy?

A vineyard in the Yarra Valley. A very fertile area in Victoria (Australia), producing amazing food produce and wines. Pinot Noir in particular

If you could have one superpower, what would it be?

I'm not into superpowers, just good health and sharing ideas.

What is your most unusual food/wine combination that you would recommend?

Arak and Kibbeh Nayee. Arak is a distilled aniseed drink very alcoholic 55% and Kibbee Nayee is the national dish of Lebanon, raw ground lamb with cracked wheat and spices. The alcohol in Arak kills the bacteria in the raw lamb.

What is the biggest myth about famous chefs/restaurants?

Getting up at 6 am to make breakfast for staff or going to the market at 3 am to buy produce for their restaurant.

Do you have a funny anecdote about a meal/dish that went wrong?

Slicing ox tongue after it's been pickled and smoked. It was inedible! You normally poach it for a few hours then serve sliced.

How do you relax outside of cooking?

Music, whisky and my partner.

What advice would you have for your 21-year-old self?

Travel, honesty, integrity, respect .

How would you like to be remembered?

Contributing to changing the course of Middle Eastern food.

10 QUICK-FIRE QUESTIONS

Roxanne Lange

HEAD CHEF, *CLOS MAGGIORE*, LONDON, UK
MOST ROMANTIC RESTAURANTS IN THE WORLD 2016

ARTIST OR ENGINEER?
ARTIST

STARTER OR DESSERT?
STARTER

APERITIF OR DIGESTIF?
APERITIF

BOOK, TV OR TABLET?
BOOK

SPRING, SUMMER, AUTUMN OR WINTER?
SPRING

SEASIDE, MOUNTAIN, CITY OR COUNTRYSIDE?
SEASIDE

STILL OR SPARKLING?
STILL

FICTION OR NON-FICTION?
NON-FICTION

MUSIC OR SILENCE?
SILENCE

SIGHT, SOUND, SMELL, TASTE OR TOUCH?
TASTE & SMELL

Magnus Ek

HEAD CHEF, *OAXEN KROG*, STOCKHOLM, SWEDEN
2 MICHELIN STARS

If you were to die and come back as an ingredient, what would it be?

Lemon geranium, I just love the flavour.

You take one year off to go travelling around the world to discover new cuisines? What is your itinerary of 2–3 countries?

I would go to Japan and stay there for quite some time. I never been there and the country and food culture seams so fascinating.

What is the best advice you've been given that has helped you along the way?

Always try to improve your dishes; even if you sometimes find that it can't be improved, it helps you to come up with new ideas.

Who are the four people you'd dream about having dinner with?

I like to eat with my friends.

What was your most memorable meal as a customer in another restaurant than your own?

I ate some fantastic sea food at a food stand in old Mazatlán Mexico 1991 and I can still remember what we had and especially some raw clams we ate with just some lime juice; it was just fantastic.

Is there something nobody knows about you/your restaurant?
Or something people don't realise?

I make most of the wood work in the restaurant as in spoons, plates, trolleys and such.

If you were not a chef/restaurateur, what profession would you like to have learnt?

I would have been a wood worker

You are given (unlimited) funds to acquire a vineyard of your choice? Which one would you buy?

I think I would buy a fruit farm. Apples or pears or plums and I would make mead and jam and marmalade instead.

If you could have one superpower, what would it be?

To be able to talk with the trees and plants.

How do you relax outside of cooking?

I take my paddle board and go paddling In the archipelago, or make some wood work.

What advice would you have for your 21-year-old self?

Realise than there is always more than one way to almost everything.

How would you like to be remembered?

As kind and helping person.

Victor Lugger

FOUNDER, *BIG MAMMA TRATTORIA*, PARIS, FRANCE AND LONDON, UK

BIG MAMMA TRATTORIA IN PARIS AND 3 RESTAURANTS IN LONDON
(GLORIA, CIRCOLO AND AVE MARIO)

You take one year off to go travelling around the world to discover new foods and wines? What is your itinerary of 2–3 countries?

I would go back to France (I currently live in London). I would travel by foot and tour the country inside out, working for a week here and a week there for the old small artisans in each town. In the city of Strasbourg where I come from, it would mean the pastry shops of Patrick and Christian, the meat shop of Frick-Lutz and cheese from Lorho. But also Roellinger in Bretagne, charcuteries in Lyon, etc.

Who are the four people you'd dream about having dinner with?

Having dinner is about how the display of generosity on the table creates bonds.

The first dinner is with my friends Sammi, Alexis and Pierre: one is the best cook, one is the most passionate about food and one is the most generous host

The second dinner is one I host to celebrate a wedding anniversary with my wife, and we have 200 people. Rules are: everyone is disguised, no table plan (the definition of horror to me), all dishes are served in big plates. But really, everyone is drunk at 6pm.

What was your most memorable food/drink pairing in a restaurant?

Margaux 1985 and paella at my grandparents'. I was born in 1984 but it was a bad year in Bordeaux. My grandfather bought 12 bottles of Margaux 1985 (a great year) and we would open one bottle a year for my birthday. This is how my family taught me to taste, respect and appreciate great products. And we would have it with paella, which is unorthodox, but my grandma cooks it to perfection and all perfect wines match all perfect dishes.

Is there something nobody knows about you? Or something people don't realise?

People have different characters. Mine is 110% transparency : you get what you see. It is faster that way to avoid people with whom there is not going to be a fit.

If you were not working in the food and wine industry, what profession would you like to have learnt?

Being a teacher is probably the closest second choice.

What is your most unusual food/drink combination that you would recommend?

Coffee and camembert and toasted croissant. It's an all time winner!

What is the biggest myth about prestigious wines?

That you have a better time with them but everything then becomes around the wine. I would rather have a good simple Nebbiolo for 30€ than a Bâtard-Montrachet, because it is very enjoyable, and doesn't take all the attention.

How do you relax outside of work?

I travel, box, do Pilates, read novels. Most of that with my wife and kids.

What advice would you have for your 21-year-old self?

Funnily enough, when I was 21, I had left home and all my parents' friends, weirdly, at some point or another, looked at me with a sort of gravity or sadness in their eyes and said: 'Make sure you enjoy these years'. Because they all said that I thought... that must be a thing so I did, and I am glad I did.

What surprising wine/spirit do you have in your wine cellar?

Mirabelle Eau de Vie from Lorraine and Vin Jaune 2011. Lots of it.

10 QUICK-FIRE QUESTIONS

Ana Roš

HEAD CHEF,
HIŠA FRANKO,
SLOVENIA

2 MICHELIN STARS

ARTIST OR ENGINEER?
ARTIST

STARTER OR DESSERT?
STARTER

APERITIF OR DIGESTIF?
APERITIF

BOOK, TV OR TABLET?
BOOK

SPRING, SUMMER, AUTUMN OR WINTER?
SPRING

SEASIDE, MOUNTAIN, CITY OR COUNTRYSIDE?
SEASIDE

STILL OR SPARKLING?
STILL

FICTION OR NON-FICTION?
FICTION

MUSIC OR SILENCE?
SILENCE

SIGHT, SOUND, SMELL, TASTE OR TOUCH?
TOUCH

Susur Lee

CELEBRITY CHEF, *SUSUR LEE RESTAURANT GROUP*, TORONTO, CANADA
LEE, LEE KITCHEN, KID LEE (ALL TORONTO) AND TUNGLOK HEEN
(SINGAPORE), WINNER OF TOP CHEF MASTERS

If you were to die and come back as an ingredient, what would it be?

I would come back as garlic. It's one of the most universal ingredients which means it's in most things... which means I would get to enjoy all cuisines for the rest of time!

You take one year off to go travelling around the world to discover new cuisines? What is your itinerary of 2–3 countries?

It's hard to narrow it down to one year... If I had the opportunity, I would do a tour of Asia. My top picks would be China, Thailand & Japan. The food there is unparalleled and there's so much to learn from region to region and many people to meet and eat with! I might never come back!

What is the best advice you've been given that has helped you along the way?

This advice might seem like it just relates to my time in the kitchen but I apply it to my everyday life: Do your best, be consistent, stay organized & keep attention to detail.

Who are the four people you'd dream about having dinner with?

My family... hands down. My sons Levi, Kai & Jet, and my wife Brenda. We always have fun and great conversations. My sons have started cooking more so this dream dinner would be them cooking for me!

What was your most memorable meal as a customer in another restaurant than your own?

A few years ago, my sons and I visited the oldest soba restaurant in Japan right after we'd spent the day learning about how soba is made. It was such a great day and the meal was a perfect way to end it!

Is there something nobody knows about you/your restaurant? Or something people don't realise?

I love yoga. I practice every day. It's a great way to still my mind from the busy energy of the restaurant.

If you were not a chef/restaurateur, what profession would you like to have learnt?

I've always been curious about learning the guitar.

If you could have one superpower, what would it be?

To live forever of course!

What is your most unusual food/wine combination that you would recommend?

I can't say I'm a big wine aficionado but I think one of my favourite unusual combinations would be Alsatian wine with Chinese food. The bright wine is a nice complement to the richness of Chinese food.

What is the biggest myth about famous chefs/restaurants?

That it's glamourous! Also... that we eat a lot. Most chefs barely have time to eat!

Do you have a funny anecdote about a meal/dish that went wrong?

Many years ago when I was first starting as a chef, I made fish en papillotte for a table. When I went back to ask how they'd enjoyed it, the man at the table raved about how good it was and that he had never had anything like it. And I believed him... because when I looked down... he'd eaten the paper!

How do you relax outside of cooking?

In addition to yoga, I walk my dog twice a day for at least 3 hours. Even though cooking for my family is still cooking, I would count it as something that I can relax doing, it's almost nourishing.

What advice would you have for your 21-year-old self?

Eat and travel... and then repeat. Tasting is how you learn and travelling is a great way to learn about yourself and the world.

How would you like to be remembered?

As someone who was inventive and great at what I did.

Eady Timms

ROOT, *HYTHE*, UK

PRIVATE CHEF AND OWNER OF ROOT, VEGAN AND VEGETARIAN CAFE

If you were to die and come back as an ingredient, what would it be?

I would choose turmeric because it adds an amazing flavour and colour to food and reminds me of sunshine. I always get organic turmeric whenever possible because I think it has a better flavour and deeper colour.

You take one year off to go travelling around the world to discover new cuisines? What is your itinerary of 2-3 countries?

Italy. Thailand and India. I love to use spices and Asian flavours in my cooking so I would love to be able to explore India and Thailand to discover new dishes which I haven't tried before. I would also choose Italy as I have been a few times and have found the produce there to be amazing quality with so much flavour. It seems that countries with more sun throughout the year produce vegetables with more intense flavours—especially if you buy them directly from local growers or farmers!

What is the best advice you've been given that has helped you along the way?

It is to experiment with different flavour combinations as it allows you to discover new dishes, which you may not have thought of before. It's probably the most time consuming, frustrating but also fun part of my job. I spend days sometimes just trying to perfect the most balanced and delicious flavours for a dish. It's good to not be afraid to experiment.

Who are the four people you'd dream about having dinner with?

Harold McGee; David Attenborough; Greta Thunberg and Jean-Michel Basquiat. I would choose these four people as I think it would be an interesting mix of food science, art and talking about environmental matters. I'm quite shy naturally so would probably prefer to stay in the kitchen or moving from the kitchen to the dining room throughout the meal. It's easier to talk and more relaxing if I'm cooking whilst I chat so maybe David and Jean could help me cook and have a glass of wine.

What was your most memorable meal as a customer in another restaurant than your own?

It was from the fish hut in Dungeness. They get fresh fish in each morning 5 minutes away from the sea. We had fish tacos which were just delicious and fresh you could tell it had just been caught that morning. We ordered the entire menu of small plates so it turned into a sort of tasting menu of everything they had on offer whilst sitting out on the beach with nothing around us for miles. Dungeness is a truly magical place.

Is there something nobody knows about you/your restaurant?
Or something people don't realise?

I am only currently open in my café Thursday, Friday and Saturday as I try to make everything I can myself. The reason I do this is to ensure that it is all made from fresh and local produce which is organic where possible. I use mainly local suppliers and as time goes on I'm constantly discovering more all the time! I'm lucky that the café is based in Kent as there is so much amazing produce right on my doorstep. A lot of cafes that I've come across buy in their cakes or savoury dishes or will buy elements such as pastry but for me it would spoil the most interesting part of owning a café: the cooking itself.

If you were not a chef/restaurateur, what profession would you like to have learnt?

I would train to be a silversmith. I have done a few courses and have loved doing it so I would make it more into a profession. It's a similar art in a way as the attention to detail has to be so important in both things.

You are given (unlimited) funds to acquire a vineyard of your choice? Which one would you buy?

I would like to make one from scratch by buying some land in Wales and trying to make a vineyard work there. I would like it to be a biodiverse nature reserve with a small holding where I would also look after animals and grow organic fruit and vegetables. At the end of the day we would sit outside cooking our home grown produce on a fire pit whilst drinking our own wine. Perfect.

If you could have one superpower, what would it be?

If I could have a super power it would be that I could turn anyone's feelings to make them happy if they were upset—I want everyone to be happy and kind to each other.

What is your most unusual food/wine combination that you would recommend?

I would recommend a chargrilled BBQ aubergine with feta, dates and pomegranate molasses served with a glass of pinot noir—amazing combination.

What is the biggest myth about famous chefs/restaurants?

A lot of restaurants / cafés that I have worked in, the environment is quite stressful and manic but I think what works best is to be in a calm and relaxed environment.

How do you relax outside of cooking?

I enjoy sewing, making wild flower jewellery and foraging but to be honest there's never a day where I don't cook. I just can't stop, the house is full of cook books that I have collected and there's nothing that I love more than curling up on the sofa in the evenings and looking through a cook book to plan what I'm cooking the next day at home or the café.

What advice would you have for your 21-year-old self?

My advice would be to take risks and not be afraid of doing something as it will always work out well in the end.

How would you like to be remembered?

As someone who brings joy to others through food.

Paul Pairet

**FOUNDER AND CHEF, *ULTRA VIOLET*, *MR & MRS BUND*,
CAFÉ POLUX, SHANGHAI, CHINA**
3 MICHELIN STARS (ULTRA VIOLET)

If you were to die and come back as an ingredient, what would it be?

A pinch of salt... to exhaust anything; a crack of pepper to lift the salt; a squeeze of lemon to zing it all.

You take one year off to go travelling around the world to discover new cuisines? What is your itinerary of 2–3 countries?

Northern Europe (Denmark) or South America (Chile or any country) because I never went there and they have driven the New World Cuisine. In any case, having travelled quite a lot professionally, it is always very interesting to dig into any food culture—there is a lot to learn anywhere.

What is the best advice you've been given that has helped you along the way?

Believe in what you cook if you want anyone to believe in it.

Who are the four people you'd dream about having dinner with?

Antonin Careme; Auguste Escoffier; Alain Chapel; Alain Ducasse. The 4 'A's ('les quatre as' en Français, 'the four aces' in English). For the obvious reason that they are or have been geniuses of their time, and meeting them together is impossible—hence a dream. And yes sometimes, I think about things that are not related to cooking... sometimes.

What was your most memorable meal as a customer in another restaurant than your own?

There has been quite a few striking meals: from my first

'fine dining' experience at 'La Tour d'Argent',Robuchon in the 80's; my first real Chinese meal in Hong Kong Shangri La in the early 90's to elBulli in late 90's... or Asador Etxebarri not so long ago... and quite a few fantastic contemporary chefs and places.

But if I had only one to extract, I would probably remember the first restaurant where I invited my young girlfriend of the time and paid with my own money that I made over the summer Job. I was so proud! I was 15, it was in Marseille in the infamous 'L'Entrecote' where we had: a Rib Eye (Entrecote) with its 'secret sauce' and a simple lettuce... What else?

Is there something nobody knows about you/your restaurant? Or something people don't realise?

Probably... and nobody knows because I won't tell ;-)

If you were not a chef/restaurateur, what profession would you like to have learnt?

I certainly love architecture... and on a similar line, I could love to design aesthetic and useful objects...

You are given (unlimited) funds to acquire a vineyard of your choice? Which one would you buy?

Probably a nice vineyard close to Perpignan—which is my native place and where they are now doing some great structured wines.

If you could have one superpower, what would it be?

Superman in a Kryptonite free world where I would not have to wear a mask and apply for a visa to end up in quarantine (where I am writing those lines by the way).

What is your most unusual food/wine combination that you would recommend?

A Rosé de Provence 'Piscine' (with a nice cube of ice) on a Tuna Sashimi. Rosé wines are too often under-rated. Or on another level... the same Rosé on the beautiful 'Blanquette de Veau' from my mum: I tried, it is a terrible clash but you need to experience the worst to understand the best.

What is the biggest myth about famous chefs/restaurants?

The morning market with a basket shaking and with the suppliers all in one spot: this is mostly TV stuff

Do you have a funny anecdote about a meal/dish that went wrong?

Rarely. Because I do not improvise for customers. But I remember the first meal I cooked for Mr Ducasse in the Café Mosaic in Paris. We wanted to do it so well; but for a reason that still escape me, a piece of broken plastic box came back from the Tubular Cucumber that he took as a starter... what a shame. He never complained and invited me for a coffee a few days after.

How do you relax outside of cooking?

I go to restaurants

What advice would you have for your 21-year-old self?

Stay put... growing older is not as good as you think.

How would you like to be remembered?

As the chef who did Ultraviolet

Dominique Crenn

HEAD CHEF, *ATELIER CRENN*, SAN FRANCISCO, USA

3 MICHELIN STARS

If you were to die and come back as an ingredient, what would it be?

Love. To spread goodness on everything and everyone.

You take one year off to go travelling around the world to discover new cuisines? What is your itinerary of 2–3 countries?

Africa, Russia, and Iceland. I love exploring new cuisines and cultures and have yet to visit these amazing places with such a rich history.

What is the best advice you've been given that has helped you along the way?

My father told me when I was young, 'You are no better than anybody, and nobody is better than you.'

Who are the four people you'd dream about having dinner with?

Greta Thunberg, Jacinda Ardern, Angela Merkel, Maya Angelou, Ruth Bader Ginsberg. I love to learn from these strong women who have had such an impact on the world.

What was your most memorable meal as a customer in another restaurant than your own?

My most memorable meals were in Tokyo. My first trip there was such an eye-opening experience of flavour combinations and interesting ingredients. There are too many restaurants to name!

Is there something nobody knows about you/your restaurant? Or something people don't realise?

I was a ballerina until the age of 9 but I didn't like it.

If you were not a chef/restaurateur, what profession would you like to have learnt?

Photography.

You are given (unlimited) funds to acquire a vineyard of your choice? Which one would you buy?

A Rosé vineyard in Bandol.

If you could have one superpower, what would it be?

I would make everyone feel that they are equal no matter their race, sex, culture, or religion—we are all human.

What is your most unusual food/wine combination that you would recommend?

Blue cheese and dark chocolate.

What is the biggest myth about famous chefs/restaurants?

That we make a lot of money.

Do you have a funny anecdote about a meal/dish that went wrong?

I can't think of anything in particular but there is a lot of trial and error in our research and development—that's one of my favourite parts of creating dishes.

How do you relax outside of cooking?

At my house in Los Angeles, looking at the hills, cooking for my friends in our library and then relaxing in the hot tub with rosé.

What advice would you have for your 21-year-old self?

Be confident, keep going, and know yourself.

How would you like to be remembered?

As someone that used her platform to make sure positive changes happen in the world for the good of humanity. I do not want to be remembered as only a Michelin star chef.

10 QUICK-FIRE QUESTIONS

Mark Hastings

GENERAL MANAGER, *CITY SOCIAL*, *JASON ATHERTON*, LONDON, UK
PREVIOUSLY DIRECTOR/GM AT DINNER BY HESTON BLUMENTHAL,
BAR BOULUD AND HAKKASAN

ARTIST OR ENGINEER?
ARTIST

STARTER OR DESSERT?
STARTER

APERITIF OR DIGESTIF?
APERITIF

BOOK, TV OR TABLET?
BOOK

SPRING, SUMMER, AUTUMN OR WINTER?
SUMMER

SEASIDE, MOUNTAIN, CITY OR COUNTRYSIDE?
SEASIDE

STILL OR SPARKLING?
SPARKLING

FICTION OR NON-FICTION?
FICTION

MUSIC OR SILENCE?
SILENCE

SIGHT, SOUND, SMELL, TASTE OR TOUCH?
TASTE

Eduard Xatruch, Mateu Casanas, Oriol Castro

CO-FOUNDERS, *COMPARTIR* (CADAQUES),
DISFRUTAR (BARCELONA) SPAIN
2 MICHELIN STARS (DISFRUTAR)

If you were to die and come back as an ingredient, what would it be?

It would be salt, because it lasts a long time and has the ability to change the kitchen.

You take one year off to go travelling around the world to discover tnew cuisines? What is your itinerary of 2-3 countries?

It would be great... First of all we will do a journey around Spain, our country, to know well the Spanish cuisine. And then, it would be great to start this travel around the world in Morocco and the Middle East (for its different cuisine, but with references in our cuisine); then stop in France (for its grand classic cuisine).

Then we could continue in Italy, Greece, Turkey... And then Asia: Thailand, India, for their special tastes; China, that is one of the richest cuisines in the world; South Korea and Japan, for the way they have to treat the product; we would also like to visit Russia (for its different ways to cook) and North and South America, especially Perú, Mexico, Chile or Argentina... It would be a dream...

What is the best advice you've been given that has helped you along the way?

Try to be better every day, in all aspects.

Who are the 4 people you'd dream about having dinner with?

We would like to have a dinner with Apicius, Carème, Escoffier and Brazier, because all of them are historical cooks that we cannot meet and it would be amazing to talk with them about what they think about the cuisine and why they did what they did.

What was your most memorable meal as a customer in another restaurant than your own?

The first time we went to together to eat to El Celler de Can Roca, because it is one of the best restaurants in the world and because the Roca brothers always have been a personal and professional reference for us. We really appreciate them.

Is there something nobody know s about you/your restaurant? Or something people don't realise?

Maybe people don't know that to offer a lunch or dinner for 40 guests, we are 65 workers in the team, doing all our best to give them one of their best experiences.

If you were not a chef/restaurateur, what profession would you like to have learnt?

I would like to have learnt to be a Catalan peasant farmer.

You are given (unlimited) funds to acquire a vineyard of your choice? Which one would you buy?

Gramona. For their quality, their passion, for the way they treat the vineyard...

If you could have one superpower, what would it be?

It would be not to make mistakes.

What is your most unusual food/wine combination that you would recommend?

We would recommend a dish of bushmeat combined with a Palo Cortado (Jerez wine). People thinks that Jerez is a wine for appetizers or for dessert, but it combines perfectly with bushmeat.

Do you have a funny anecdote about a meal/dish that went wrong?

Yes, we have. Sometimes, you try to do something that you think will be a great idea and then the result is very bad... And it was what happened when we discovered our own technique 'panchino'. We were trying to do something very different, it didn't work, but we 'discovered' this new technique.

How do you relax outside of cooking?

Spending time with my daughters.

What advice would you have for your 21-year-old self?

My self-advice will be to live in the moment more.

How would you like to be remembered?

I would like to be remembered for being a good person.

Debbie Fadul

FOUNDER AND CHEF, *DIACA*, GUATEMALA CITY, GUATEMALA
FOUNDER OF MON COEUR, DIACA, EN RESTAURANTE AND CRECE EN GUATE

If you were to die and come back as an ingredient, what would it be?

As a Chiltepe, a pure, small green humble, unique flourish spice flavour, high energy, sweet-strong, amazing for your gut, tiny chilli from our Guatemala.

You take one year off to go travelling around the world to discover new cuisines? What is your itinerary of 2–3 countries?

America; because each country has such rich soils, amazing history and connection to nature in such different and similar ways

What is the best advice you've been given that has helped you along the way?

Always concentrate on why you're doing what you're doing.

Who are the four people you'd dream about having dinner with?

Rudolf Steiner, Marius Schneider, Michael Pollan and my Grandmother. I admire how each of them sees nature, and what we can learn from her. Talking different points of views but at the same time, everything will connect and teach us that everything is connected and we need to embrace that to have a perfect symbiosis with each other and nature.

What was your most memorable meal as a customer in another restaurant than your own?

The perfect chicharron in Quito's Market and Palm Tree Warms filled with White Cacao in Yasuni Reserve Community in Ecuatorian Amazon.

Is there something nobody knows about you/your restaurant? Or something people don't realise?

That I have a very sensitive tongue and nose and that most of the time I don't say everything that I sense in my surroundings.

If you were not a chef/restaurateur, what profession would you like to have learnt?

Biologist or anthropologist.

You are given (unlimited) funds to acquire a vineyard of your choice? Which one would you buy?

I wouldn't buy a vineyard I would buy a MILPA, filled with endemic corns and amaranth and if I made a drink, it would be beer with the amaranth and whisky with the corn.

If you could have one superpower, what would it be?

It will be to feel when you eat, the same extreme way as I feel when I see, taste, touch and cook

What is your most unusual food/wine combination that you would recommend?

Spicy Tamale Masa with red Oysters coffee chimichurri, white chocolate and crispy red chorizo with a Cacique Maravilla Gutiflower Moscatel Corinto.

What is the biggest myth about famous chefs/restaurants?

'You can find good food only here'. Good food is everywhere, good ingredients with respect equals good food.

Do you have a funny anecdote about a meal/dish that went wrong?

In one of our restaurants, we had a dish with wheatgrass; we told our maitre that it was very important that he put only the leaves, not the roots. At the end of service, we saw that everybody uploaded photos of the dish saying that wheatgrass roots were amazing!

How do you relax outside of cooking?

Going to farms and climbing volcanos.

What advice would you have for your 21-year-old self?

That everything that you do, do it with a light heart, pure mind and respect the why in everything. A light heart so you are humble, a pure mind so you cook real and respect so you make good symbiosis with man and nature.

How would you like to be remembered?

As someone that felt everything in complete gratefulness, so strong that her energy made you realise yours and see how blessed we are with so little.

Jane Beedle

BAKER, KENT, UK
GREAT BRITISH BAKE OFF FINALIST

If you were to die and come back as an ingredient, what would it be?

This may sound super bland but bring me back as vanilla. Everyone loves it and it gets to go to loads of parties.

You take one year off to go travelling around the world to discover new cuisines? What is your itinerary of 2–3 countries?

To take a year off and discover new cuisines would be a real treat. I'd start in India as I just love Indian food but am absolutely rubbish at getting the flavours right. There are so many different regional foods I could spend a year there and still not experience everything. My second choice would be China, again so much to learn and so many different regional dishes, although I don't think I would be good with chicken feet, I have a thing about feathers and feet.

What is the best advice you've been given that has helped you along the way?

My Dad told me 'never give up'. If you get knocked back then pick yourself up and try again. I got my optimism from my Dad.

Who are the four people you'd dream about having dinner with?

Aside from my family who are always my number one dinner guests:

Graham Norton because he is funny and brings out the best in people.

Joan Rivers, she would be hysterically funny and probably wouldn't eat all the puddings.

Claudia Winkleman just because I love her

Chris Hemsworth just because...

What was your most memorable meal as a customer in another restaurant than your own?

It was in a tiny restaurant somewhere in the middle of France. We needed somewhere to stay and pulled up at a very dusty looking place that was offering rooms. Through two huge gates was the most gorgeous courtyard filled with geraniums. The dessert was the most delicious crème caramel, quite the best I've ever tasted. I still think of it many years on. I'm salivating at the thought.

Is there something nobody knows about you/your restaurant? Or something people don't realise?

Yes there is and it's staying that way!

If you were not a chef/restaurateur, what profession would you like to have learnt?

Baking is my third/fourth career so I've had a chance to try many things and I have at last found my great love but I would like to learn pottery and may start that after lockdown. My other great love is Egypt, I think I would have liked to be an archaeologist.

You are given (unlimited) funds to acquire a vineyard of your choice? Which one would you buy?

I don't drink so not the question for me really but basically any one would do my husband is not too choosy.

If you could have one superpower, what would it be?

That would be easy, I would be able to point at litter

and it would end up in the offenders' bed.

Do you have a funny anecdote about a meal/dish that went wrong?

There are too many to mention.

How do you relax outside of cooking?

Dog walking, spending time with friends, gardening and generally being out of doors.

What advice would you have for your 21-year-old self?

Follow your dream, happiness is more important than money and ignore the doubters.

How would like to be retmembered?

For being kind. I don't always manage it but it's what I strive for.

Laurent David

HEAD CHEF, *LOU PESCADOU*, LONDON, UK
LEGENDARY FRENCH RESTAURANT IN EARL'S COURT

If you were to die and come back as an ingredient, what would it be?

Rice because it can feed the world, it's not expensive, easy to find and to cook.

You take one year off to go travelling around the world to discover new cuisines? What is your itinerary of 2–3 countries?

I would go to Thailand, Argentina and certainly China. These three countries seem interesting in terms of food and spices.

What is the best advice you've been given that has helped you along the way?

At the beginning of my career, a lot of chefs told me 'you are not cooking for you but for the pleasure of the clients, never forget it'. I also remember being told that cooking for someone was 'a way of showing love'.

Who are the four people you'd dream about having dinner with?

Georges Brassens, Jacques Brel, Louis Amstrong and Sammy Davis Junior because they say in words what I try to express in food and I'm sure they are full-hearted people.

What was your most memorable meal as a customer in another restaurant than your own?

That would be at Pierre Kauffman's (La Tante Claire); everything was just perfect: pieds de cochons farcis, scallops and soufflé à la pistache. The meal, the service and the moment with friends was my best memory of a meal.

Is there something nobody knows about you/your restaurant? Or something people don't realise?

Most people don't know that cooking is hard work, lots of hours, get up early, physically tiring, tense service, finishing late...

If you were not a chef/restaurateur, what profession would you like to have learnt?

I would have loved to be an actor, singer or rugby player... but those are just dreams, my work as a chef has been my only passion and still is.

You are given (unlimited) funds to acquire a vineyard of your choice? Which one would you buy?

I would like to own a big 'Bourgogne' name because they are my favourite to taste!

If you could have one superpower, what would it be?

I would have the ability to learn very fast, open a book and get the knowledge straight away!

What is the biggest myth about famous chefs/restaurants?

We often see famous chefs as tyrannic people but in fact most of them want to please everybody and it is tough...

Do you have a funny anecdote about a meal/dish that went wrong?

Once at Twickenham (before an England vs All Blacks

game), I served some 'eclairs' that were still frozen (and didn't realise) and after the game, supporters from New Zealand asked me if I had some more ice creams...

How do you relax outside of cooking?

When I had the chance to have a day off, I slept all through the day.

What advice would you have for your 21-year-old self?

Travel around the world to learn more about cooking.

How would you like to be remembered?

I don't really care about fame or anything, what really matters is pleasure, life experiences... and I just hope I gave some kind of happiness or good moments with my cooking.

10 QUICK-FIRE QUESTIONS

Enrique Olvera

HEAD CHEF, *PUJOL*, MEXICO CITY, MEXICO

7 CONSECUTIVE YEARS IN THE WORLD'S 50 BEST RESTAURANTS

ARTIST OR ENGINEER?
ARTIST

STARTER OR DESSERT?
STARTER

APERITIF OR DIGESTIF?
DIGESTIF

BOOK, TV OR TABLET?
BOOK

SPRING, SUMMER, AUTUMN OR WINTER?
SPRING

SEASIDE, MOUNTAIN, CITY OR COUNTRYSIDE?
MOUNTAIN

STILL OR SPARKLING?
SPARKLING

FICTION OR NON-FICTION?
FICTION

MUSIC OR SILENCE?
MUSIC

SIGHT, SOUND, SMELL, TASTE OR TOUCH?
THIS IS A HARD ONE, I CAN'T CHOOSE

Gio Renzo Fioraso

PRIVATE CHEF, UK / ITALY

If you were to die and come back as an ingredient, what would it be?

I guess I would love to be a potato: it is just perfect, one of my favourite ingredients; since it was discovered, it helped so many people to survive, it can grow easily and in a relative small environment. It tastes just amazing, fried, boiled, braised, oven baked grilled and slow cooked; you will never go wrong with a potato.... What about a great mash potatoes cream? I think it is just a peace of heaven! The only bad thing about reviving as a potato, I guess my life will be quite short and I will be eaten pretty soon, no?

You take one year off to go travelling around the world to discover new cuisines? What is your itinerary of 2-3 countries?

I will start in South America (perhaps Peru) then move to Mexico and finally Canada, trying to understand as much as possible their ingredients and their own way to create food.

What is the best advice you've been given that has helped you along the way?

Quite recently a great chef explained to me how important to have volume in a dish, to grow in height and not only on a flat dimension; it is the same concept as with flavours, you need more than one for make something unique.

Who are the four people you'd dream about having dinner with?

I can imagine myself having a meal with Auguste Escoffier, Gualtiero Marchesi, Anthony Bourdain and Rudy Kurniawan. I would have very little to contribute to the conversation but I would have a lot to listen to and learn. It would be the best set up to put side by side traditions, origins and rules but also the excitement of the new wave and the willingness to overcome barriers.

What was your most memorable meal as a customer in another restaurant than your own?

So far it is probably Osteria Francescana of Massimo Bottura, those 6 hours spent there were not all about food, but much more: you realise that the food industry right now is not the same at it was 60 or 80 years ago; we don't eat food for survive; right now, we eat for pleasure, it is more a philosophical approach to life than anything else, at least for me.

Is there something nobody knows about you/your restaurant? Or something people don't realise?

I guess almost nobody knows that when I was young I wasn't interested in food; more than that I wasn't eating at all: the time for the meal for me was the worst part of the day, I couldn't enjoy that, it was just time that I was losing instead of doing something else. Now I realise the importance of having time to sit down and enjoy a proper meal, to give some time to yourself to appreciate simple things like life, our surroundings, the extreme importance of seasons and the magic flavours of every single ingredient that we touch.

If you were not a chef/restaurateur, what profession would you like to have learnt?

There are few of them, but after food, wine is my second passion, so I would have loved since an early age to be able of spend time with a wine producer, learning about different grapes and understanding the magic secret of this beautiful violet (or other colours) liquid.

You are given (unlimited) funds to acquire a vineyard of your choice? Which one would you buy?

The best option for me would be somewhere that nobody has done before, so I wouldn't buy an existing vineyard, but perhaps I would buy a large farm or piece of land and slowly start to plant vines and see if I can create something interesting and unique, possibly in the Rioja region, one of my favourite in the world.

If you could have one superpower, what would it be?

I would love to wake up one day with the Psychokinesis super power, and being able to cook and plate a dish just using the power of my mind and not my hands.

What is your most unusual food/wine combination that you would recommend?

There are a few combinations that I think are unusual but I really enjoy: recently I paired a pigeon breast with a light Chablis and it worked perfectly, or at least I loved it. In the future, I really would like to start and pair each single dish to a specific song, not just wine but much more.

What is the biggest myth about famous chefs/restaurants?

Most of people think that famous chefs are something close to a god or a superhero, and from one point of view they probably are, but under their name, there is always a simple person, who works hard, most of the days of their life without having a lot of free time, using all their love and effort to make other people happy; for them. Cooking is not an act of fame, but a way to express love and emotion.

Do you have a funny anecdote about a meal/dish that went wrong?

I remember few years ago, I was cooking for a party of 20 people, and when I got there, only one hob was actually working, so I ended up cooking almost all the menu in the oven, as it was the only thing working properly in the kitchen; for sure, it wasn't one of my best meals, but at least I managed to serve food.

How do you relax outside of cooking?

My best option to relax after cooking is a good day playing golf; when I am playing, I can really switch off my brain from work and only focus on the game.

What advice would you have for your 21-year-old self?

Find something that you really like, something that you are happy and comfortable with; if you manage to find that, follow it with passion and it will be your career in the future.

How would you like to be remembered?

As someone who always tried to improve, to do better, learn from mistakes, work on them and push harder than before.

Rasmus Munk

CHEF AND CO-OWNER, *ALCHEMIST*, DENMARK
2 MICHELIN STARS, 2020 AND 2021 "RESTAURANT OF THE YEAR"
IN WHITE GUIDE DENMARK

If you were to die and come back as an ingredient, what would it be?

A fugu fish. So I could at least end my days in the hands of a trained professional.

You take one year off to go travelling around the world to discover new cuisines? What is your itinerary of 2–3 countries?

Japan, South Africa, India. I long to dive deeper in these regional cuisines.

What is the best advice you've been given that has helped you along the way?

Be humble and don't forget where you come from.

Who are the four people you'd dream about having dinner with?

Aristotle, Ferran Adrià, Andy Warhol, Auguste Escoffier.

What was your most memorable meal as a customer in another restaurant than your own?

Sugita in Tokyo. Uniquely layered flavours on an extremely high level.

Is there something nobody knows about you / your restaurant? Or something people don't realise?

Yes. That's all I'm gonna say 😊

If you were not a chef / restaurateur, what profession would you like to have learnt?

Designer or engineer.

You are given (unlimited) funds to acquire a vineyard of your choice? Which one would you buy?

DRC. Why not?

If you could have one superpower, what would it be?

Green Lanterns ring.

What is the biggest myth about famous chefs/restaurants?

That we all shout and rage in the kitchen.

Do you have a funny anecdote about a meal / dish that went wrong?

I don't know how funny it was at the time, but when I was trying to figure out how I could serve cow's udder in the restaurant (butchers usually throw it away). I got an udder from a farmer and put it in my car. While I was driving, the milk rose to the teats and began to spray everywhere. Drenched completely, I came up with the idea to serve the udder so that the guests can watch the liquid, which will later become the sauce, pour out. But when we began the experiment, we didn't take into account how sensitive to bacteria the udders were and many of us who sampled it became quite sick. One of the chefs had to be taken to hospital, and the others were out of action for a couple of weeks.

How do you relax outside of cooking?

Dining at other restaurants.

What advice would you have for your 21-year-old self?

Try not to care too much about what other people think.

How would you like to be remembered?

I would rather be remembered as someone who made an impression on the world and changed the way we think about gastronomy than being the chef who gathered the most accolades, stars and prizes.

10 QUICK-FIRE QUESTIONS

ARTIST OR ENGINEER?
ARTIST

STARTER OR DESSERT?
STARTER

APERITIF OR DIGESTIF?
APERITIF

BOOK, TV OR TABLET?
TV

SPRING, SUMMER, AUTUMN OR WINTER?
SPRING

SEASIDE, MOUNTAIN, CITY OR COUNTRYSIDE?
SEASIDE

STILL OR SPARKLING?
SPARKLING

FICTION OR NON-FICTION?
FICTION

MUSIC OR SILENCE?
MUSIC

SIGHT, SOUND, SMELL, TASTE OR TOUCH?
TASTE

WINEMAKERS

VINEYARD OWNERS

Sandrine Garbay

MAITRE DE CHAI, *CHATEAU D'YQUEM*, SAUTERNES

You take one year off to go travelling around the world to discover new foods and wines? What is your itinerary of 2-3 countries?

First Italy and specifically Tuscany and Piemonte which I have never visited. Italian food has a well deserved reputation for being extraordinary and its famous wines are among the best in the world.

Then I would travel to South America to discover Argentinian and Chilean wines. I have never been to the Andes—such a mythical place with incredible sceneries.

Finally I would like to go to the home of wine origins—Georgia. The first traces of vine growing and wine making there go back 8,000 years. Some of their traditional methods have remained and I would be very moved to immerse myself in this universe.

What is the best advice you've been given that has helped you along the way?

My dad kept repeating throughout my childhood: 'work is health'. At the time, I didn't find the advice much fun but looking back, I can see that working really is an integral part to a balanced life. It allows you to gain confidence in yourself, to have a purpose, to help you navigate through difficult life moments. Obviously it requires a job that you flourish in. My own work, which I'm passionate about, has given me a strength I didn't know I had and has been a constant source of satisfaction which are essential to my happiness. My family life is the other pillar of my happiness and I would never neglect it—it's all a matter of balance!

Who are the four people you'd dream about having dinner with?

I would love to dine with Barbara Hendricks, who I admire enormously for her voice of course but also for her great elegance and her work with the UN promoting peace in the world; she would have so many stories to share.

Then, in a completely different field, I would invite Jack Johnson in the hope that during dinner, he would sing some of the uplifting and appeasing songs which I love listening to.

I would love to have met Simone Veil so she could have told me about her fight in parliament and the French politic class in general for abortion rights. I can't begin to imagine the strength and determination she must have needed to defend this worthwhile cause

And finally, to lighten things up, I would enjoy sharing the diner with Florence Foresti, a French comedian who makes me laugh a lot!

What was your most memorable food/wine pairing in a restaurant?

I have great memories of a 'revisited beef carrots' dish paired with Yquem: Thierry Marx served this very unusual match (red meat and Yquem) at dinner and it was delicious. The gentle sweet note from the carrot was a gentle reminder of the softness of the noble rot. And the confit of beef created a really original balance with the wine. But beyond the success of the flavours, I think I was even more taken by the left field nature of the idea itself, which was great.

I consider Thierry Marx as one of the most talented chefs of his era—he displays great creativity on the plate and possesses outstanding all round general knowledge. He is always fascinating to listen to.

Is there something nobody knows about you? Or something people don't realise?

I am a fervent advocate of scientific rigor in the face of pseudo-sciences that increasingly permeate our society. You can't brush away all the progress that science has brought on the mere pretext of more natural and less science in our daily lives. I am very worried by the growing obscurantism that surrounds us; there is little room left for common sense and reason. I always encourage students I teach to use their scientific brain to be constructively critical in their assessment of the trend for alternative agricultural methods... even though they are attractive in principle (less inputs, back to ancestral values, proximity to nature), they are not founded on any scientific grounding and they exploit the seductive belief that a return to the natural is the best way forward. But beware! Science can indeed not explain everything and in that sense, it is useful to explore new ways but certainly not by radically opposing established scientific knowledge.

If you were not working in a vineyard, what profession would you like to have learnt?

I would have loved to be a psychologist—delving deep into the human soul and helping people who struggle.

As a teenager, I was very tempted by this path but in the end, my love for biochemistry and microbiology took over. I have no regrets because my job brings sunshine to people's senses and tastebuds so it is also very useful.

You are given (unlimited) funds to acquire another vineyard of your choice? Which one would you buy?

I think I would purchase Klein Constantia (in South Africa). Well, if the owners would agree to sell! I am a big fan of this wine and place: the bowl shaped vineyard facing the bay of Cape Town is breath taking. And the aromatic intensity of the wine never fails to enthuse whenever I taste it. What a place, what a wine! A sweet wine once again

If you could have one superpower, what would it be?

I would like to be able to eat and drink without worrying about its effects on my body. I am a real 'gourmande' and being watchful of what I eat is really hard!

What is your most unusual food/wine combination that you would recommend?

It would naturally be a pairing with a dessert wine—people no longer know what dish to serve those magical wines with. For example, only a few know that seafood such as lobster or scallops are a perfect match with a glass of Yquem. It's actually my favourite pairing!

What is the biggest myth about prestigious wines?

The belief that prestigious wines require a lot of technology or winemaking intervention—it's the complete opposite! Prestigious wines generally have exceptional terroirs so you just need to respect them so their quality can express itself through the grapes. The role of the winemaker is then to reveal the uniqueness of the place in the wines with the least possible intervention. Less is more!

Do you have a funny anecdote about a vintage that went wrong (or nearly went wrong)?

Usually when you struggle with a vintage, we struggle to find it amusing. But I can share my worst winemaking memory—I can laugh about it now but at the time, I was mortified: early in my career as maitre de chai at Yquem, I made a mistake in the dosing of a nutrient we add to the grape juice so fermentation goes smoothly: I put 10 times the amount I should have in a 5,000 litre vat. But thankfully we were able to use the juice to complement all the others and it actually worked out giving splendid wines! I never did that again but people say that great ideas often originate from mistakes so maybe I should meditate this thought!

How do you relax outside of work?

I have a simple life—I keep busy with my family, friends and looking after the home. I like cooking, I love sharing over a nice meal and good wines; I also like the cinema, performing arts, travelling. I force myself to exercise 2 or 3 times a week ideally—I force myself because it's not a huge passion but I know it's an important part of a healthy lifestyle and it does help.

What advice would you have for your 21-year-old self?

Don't hesitate to be assertive in work meetings; your ideas are just as good as those of your male colleagues. Be bold!

What is the grape variety (other than your own) you would have liked to work with?

I would love to work with Syrah: I am amazed by its different aromatic expressions. The famous wines of the Northern Rhone valley really impress me. And also, it'd be nice to make red wine for a change!

What surprising wine (from a different region) do you have in your wine cellar?

My husband and I have a few old vintage Jura vins jaunes, from great winemakers; those wines are incredible and really worthy of attention. But you need to be guided to really understand them; we love them!

Peter Sisseck

**OWNER AND WINEMAKER, *DOMINIO DE PINGUS*,
RIBERA DEL DUERO, SPAIN**

You take one year off to go travelling around the world to discover new foods and wines? What is your itinerary of 2–3 countries?

I would first and foremost go to China; the diversity is immense. Then South Korea (I don't think they would let me in in the northern part). It would then depend on how much I would like to travel if I go to India or Mexico.

What is the best advice you've been given that has helped you along the way?

I love books and reading but you have to practice a lot to learn a skill—like to learn to prune or make the best sauce or to build a dry stone wall.

Who are the four people you'd dream about having dinner with?

Goethe would be one and Thomas Jefferson as they both loved food and wine... Hemmingway for being a rascal... Madame de Stael so it doesn't get to masculine

What was your most memorable food/wine pairing in a restaurant?

I once had a red curry in Bangkok with a beautiful off dry (and ice-cold) Zind-Humbrecht; I can't remember the year, nor the vineyard.

Is there something nobody knows about you? Or something people don't realise?

I guess a lot... I don't think they realise I love nature and farming more than wine.

If you were not working in a vineyard, what profession would you like to have learnt?

Architect

You are given (unlimited) funds to acquire another vineyard of your choice? Which one would you buy?

It would for sure be in Europe. Some historic place with a Monastic connection and tradition.

If you could have one superpower, what would it be?

I think we all need more peace in the world, if I could help in that that would be great. But for the moment it is somebody much bigger and important who has that job

What is your most unusual food/wine combination that you would recommend?

Guillardeau no 5 Oysters topped with a dash of Beluga and my Fino from Jerez...

What is the biggest myth about prestigious wines?

The real secret is... it is all just wine.

Do you have a funny anecdote about a vintage that went wrong (or nearly went wrong)?

I don't know if is funny but the 2002 from my winery Dominio de Pingus was not a good vintage so I didn't make Pingus so I could blend it with Flor de Pingus; even that didn't help but it is still very good. Mea Culpa.

How do you relax outside of work?

Walking and reading

What advice would you have for your 21-year-old self?

Keep studying the piano, you fool.

What is the grape variety (other than your own) you would have liked to work with?

Chenin Blanc, Savagnin or Cabernet Franc from Lafleur (Pomerol).

What surprising wine (from a different region) do you have in your wine cellar?

I have a couple of Chinese wines Chateau Rongzi and the Ao Yun.

Marc Hochar

OWNER, *CHATEAU MUSAR*, BEKAA VALLEY, LEBANON

You take one year off to go travelling around the world to discover new foods and wines? What is your itinerary of 2-3 countries?

South Africa to enjoy a return to nature, experience the wilderness of that continent and their wines and food.

Italy because of the variety of their wines and food, and the friendly people

New Zealand for their amazing Pinot Noirs and to understand what it is like to live on the other side of the world.

What is the best advice you've been given that has helped you along the way?

No matter what job you decide to go for, even if you opt to become a shoe-shiner, be the best at what you do.

Who are the four people you'd dream about having dinner with?

Jesus, Alexander the Great, Lady Gaga and my late father

What was your most memorable food/wine pairing in a restaurant?

Sour cherry ice cream and fruits with Chateau Musar red 2004. Extraordinary because I never expected any of our red wines to pair well with a dessert.

Is there something nobody knows about you? Or something people don't realise?

I don't even know myself, let alone what others think they know about me!

If you were not working in a vineyard, what profession would you like to have learnt?

Architecture.

If you could have one superpower, what would it be?

Time travel or teletransportation.

What is your most unusual food/wine combination that you would recommend?

Very old dry white wine with dry-aged steak.

What is the biggest myth about prestigious wines?

That they should be expensive.

Do you have a funny anecdote about a vintage that went wrong (or nearly went wrong)?

1984 vintage of Chateau Musar red. Fermented in trucks during transport from the vineyards to the winery during the civil war, where transport lasted 5 days instead of 3 hours. Unsellable wine for the first 2 decades, but at year 30 completely blossomed and became one of the best recovery wines we've ever made.

How do you relax outside of work?

Music, skiing or doing nothing.

What advice would you have for your 21-year-old self?

Don't be too serious, enjoy your life.

What is the grape variety (other than your own) you would have liked to work with?

Nerelo Mascalese.

What surprising wine (from a different region) do you have in your wine cellar?

Tokaji.

Matt Day

WINEMAKER, *KLEIN CONSTANTIA*, CAPE TOWN

You take one year off to go travelling around the world to discover new foods and wines? What is your itinerary of 2-3 countries?

This is tough but my top 2 would be: Armenia; because I have to see Mount Ararat to see where Noah planted vines. I love the concept and would just love to go and see it. The history of the region is amazing and visiting potentially one of the oldest wine regions in the word is definitely high up there on my to do list. And St Helena; visiting where Napoleon used to enjoy our wines has always been on my bucket list.

What is the best advice you've been given that has helped you along the way?

Don't overcomplicate things. When we try too hard we often mess things up so let them happen naturally.

Who are the four people you'd dream about having dinner with?

Napoleon Bonaparte because I would love to share a glass of Vin de Constance with him and see if its meets his standard.

Didier Dagueneau. He is probably one of the greatest winemakers that ever lived. The wines that he used to make have always been a huge inspiration in my life.

Nelson Mandela. Need I say more and who wouldn't want to spend time with him.

Elon Musk, because I would like to discuss being the first person to drink Vin de Constance in space, and what an incredible person.

What was your most memorable food/wine pairing in a restaurant?

There are too many to choose from. One that I often speak about was pairing crocodile with Klein Constantia Sauvignon Blanc. It's amazing, you have to try it. The other was a 5-course meal, each course was paired with a different vintage of Vin de Constance. If you choose the right vintage the options are endless.

Is there something nobody knows about you? Or something people don't realise?

I was a Springbok Boy Scout; I am as shy as anything and I have been hit by lightning twice.

If you were not working in a vineyard, what profession would you like to have learnt?

To be honest I have no clue I love what I do but maybe a farmer, I'm not sure...

You are given (unlimited) funds to acquire another vineyard of your choice? Which one would you buy?

I would purchase LVMH. That way we will cover all the basics and there are a couple of amazing brands involved.

If you could have one superpower, what would it be?

I would like supersonic smell; just kidding I would like to read people's minds.

What is your most unusual food/wine combination that you would recommend?

Popcorn mixed with chocolate candy and red wine...

What is the biggest myth about prestigious wines?

The perception that price determines quality. The only thing that price determines is ego.

Do you have a funny anecdote about a vintage that went wrong (or nearly went wrong)?

The trick about being a good winemaker is that you just need to say anything with confidence and people will believe you. So any mistakes I make I confidently tell people that I did it on purpose. So to answer your question nothing has ever gone wrong in our cellar ever!

How do you relax outside of work?

I collect vinyls, aquascape and spend time with the family.

What advice would you have for your 21-year-old self?

Spend more time with the people that you love.

What is the grape variety (other than your own) you would have liked to work with?

Pontac, it is super rare and forms part of one of the original varietals used in the 1700's in Constantia.

What surprising wine (from a different region) do you have in your wine cellar?

None, life is too short to hold onto wine. If you have something special in your cellar you need to find an occasion to share it with friends. That being said I have an amazing collection of Vin de Constance dating back to 1991 (I can't afford anything older).

Mark Angeli

OWNER AND WINEMAKER, *FERME DE LA SANSONNIERE*,
LOIRE VALLEY, FRANCE

You take one year off to go travelling around the world to discover new foods and wines? What is your itinerary of 2–3 countries?

I will choose Spain for the treasures of old vines, Greece for the non-grafted vines and Georgia for the beginning of the story.

What is the best advice you've been given that has helped you along the way?

We are all born mad, only a few of us remain mad.

Who are the four people you'd dream about having dinner with?

J.K. Rowling to understand how she has imagined it all alone; Pierre and Jean Gonon, Jean Louis Chave and Emmanuel Reynaud together with Pierre Overnoy (the pope of "Natural wines") for their fabulous and unique wines, their humility and peasant common sense.

What was your most memorable food/wine pairing in a restaurant?

Khayyam 2005 from Mas de Libian with slow cooked boar.

Is there something nobody knows about you? Or something people don't realise?

I was a stone mason before being wine grower.

If you were not working in a vineyard, what profession would you like to have learnt?

Bakery.

You are given (unlimited) funds to acquire another vineyard of your choice? Which one would you buy?

Chateau Grillet.

If you could have one superpower, what would it be?

Planting forest everywhere.

What is your most unusual food/wine combination that you would recommend?

Sweet Rosé with spicy meals.

What is the biggest myth about prestigious wines?

The yields in renowned wine regions.

Do you have a funny anecdote about a vintage that went wrong (or nearly went wrong)?

A friend harvested rotten Chenin grapes in 2012 and the wine obtained was said by journalists to be similar to a Corton Charlemagne!

How do you relax outside of work?

Listening to and singing French songs of Léo Ferré, Allain Leprest and Claude Nougaro.

What advice would you have for your 21-year-old self?

Get up early to listen to the birds.

What is the grape variety (other than your own) you would have liked to work with?

Petit Manseng

What surprising wine (from a different region) do you have in your wine cellar?

A Japanese wine from Hokkaido made by Ken Sasaki.

Nigel Greening

OWNER, *FELTON ROAD*, CENTRAL OTAGO, NEW ZEALAND

You take one year off to go travelling around the world to discover new foods and wines? What is your itinerary of 2-3 countries?

Japan is always number 1: the most unique place on earth culturally. In culinary terms I'd add India next, then China. There is no real travel need to explore wine: wine travels easier than people and almost anything wine wise is available to explore in the UK. Exploring the culture of wine is another matter, and then it probably has to be Germany, incredibly diverse now, with great reds as well as whites to learn about.

What is the best advice you've been given that has helped you along the way?

Never fear failure. Failure teaches you so much more than success: success can happen by accident, failure always has a reason, so failure teaches you so much better. More than anything it teaches you resilience.

Who are the four people you'd dream about having dinner with?

Albert Einstein, Bertrand Russell, Mark Twain and Douglas Adams: four of the finest creators of pithy one line thoughts. Dinner isn't a long time, so you need people who can give a lot with a few words! And I think they'd all get on well with each other!

What was your most memorable food/wine pairing in a restaurant?

Drinking Provence rosé, on a beautiful terrace overlooking the sea, eating stuffed courgette flowers. Nowhere flash, just 3 definitive statements of the same place at the same time.

Is there something nobody knows about you? Or something people don't realise?

I think that somebody knows pretty much everything about me, but things most people don't know? Maybe the fact that I'm a luthier: I make guitars as a hobby.

If you were not working in a vineyard, what profession would you like to have learnt?

Probably to be a better luthier.

You are given (unlimited) funds to acquire another vineyard of your choice? Which one would you buy?

None. It will take more years than I have, to understand the land I have already. Also, it is important not to be greedy!

If you could have one superpower, what would it be?

A better palate, though flying would be cool.

What is your most unusual food/wine combination that you would recommend?

Roast new potatoes with really good Pinot Noir. Nothing else: just the potatoes, roast over charcoal in thyme and olive oil, eaten with your fingers, outdoors, on a summer's evening.

What is the biggest myth about prestigious wines?

That they are worth the silly money they command. It's just wine.

Do you have a funny anecdote about a vintage that went wrong (or nearly went wrong)?

There is nothing funny about vintages going wrong, nearly or otherwise! Any winemaker can tell you that! I do remember an incident when we were concerned about the number of earwigs in the fruit at harvest. Ladybirds produce a serious flavour taint if they get in the fruit when you pick it. We were concerned that earwigs might have a similar issue. So we conducted a tasting of crushed earwigs in both water and wine. No problem was observed. Not a great culinary discovery, though.

How do you relax outside of work?

I cook. Somewhat fanatically, I confess; but I doubt if I could live without cooking.

What advice would you have for your 21-year-old self?

Keep your word. You want to end your life having never made an enemy through your own actions.

What is the grape variety (other than your own) you would have liked to work with?

Gewurztraminer is an interesting challenge, very different to other grapes in many ways. I own about 7 Gewurtz vines, (mis-plants scattered in the vineyard), but only enough to make a little sorbet, not wine.

What surprising wine (from a different region) do you have in your wine cellar?

Quite a few. I like showing people Muxagat Os Xistos Altos: a white wine made from the Rabigato grape in Portugal. Always impressive if you get somebody who can spot it blind!

Thomas Duroux

CEO, *CHATEAU PALMER*, MARGAUX, FRANCE

You take one year off to go travelling around the world to discover new foods and wines? What is your itinerary of 2–3 countries?

Thailand. Not really for the wines but definitely for food as this probably the most refined cuisine in all Asia.

Tokyo. Nowhere else in the world you may find such a high level of knowledge in cuisine and wine.

Lima. I don't know Peru but I have been told that this is the place for wine and food in South America.

What is the best advice you've been given that has helped you along the way?

In anything you do be passionate.

Who are the four people you'd dream about having dinner with?

Keith Jarret. The greatest jazz pianist of all time.

Joel Dicker. Fabulous Swiss writer.

Pierre Soulages. 101 years old French painter.

Donald Trump. Just to see how crazy he is!

What was your most memorable food/wine pairing in a restaurant?

Back in 1996, I was a young winemaker working in Hungary.

I had the chance to be invited by the legend Alain Sanderes at his restaurant Lucas Carton in Paris. He prepared an incredible lievre a la royal (Antonin Careme recipe!!) with a Chateau de Beaucastel 1983. I'll remember that for my entire life.

If you were not working in a vineyard, what profession would you like to have learnt?

Musician or mathematics genius!

You are given (unlimited) funds to acquire another vineyard of your choice? Which one would you buy?

I would create the most remote and creasy vineyard from scratch at the top of Alicudi Island (north of Sicily).

If you could have one superpower, what would it be?

I'd make sure that French people stop complaining all the time!

What is your most unusual food/wine combination that you would recommend?

A saffron risotto with a Chateau-Chalon.

What is the biggest myth about prestigious wines?

That you have to be knowledgeable to understand them.

Do you have a funny anecdote about a vintage that went wrong (or nearly went wrong)?

2018 was a extremely challenging vintage in the vineyard because of the mildew (fungus disease) pressure. By the end of July we were convinced that the entire crop was lost. We finally saved a very small quantity of fruit and we produced what is maybe the most incredible Chateau Palmer of all time!!

How do you relax outside of work?

Listening music with a glass of wine and hiking the gorgeous Pyrénées mountains.

What advice would you have for your 21-year-old self?

Be quiet!!!

What is the grape variety (other than your own) you would have liked to work with?

Mourvèdre

What surprising wine (from a different region) do you have in your wine cellar?

A 1904 'Passereta' produced near Modena in Italy by one of my ancestors

Adrian Pikes

WINEMAKER, *WESTWELL WINES*, KENT, UNITED KINGDOM

You take one year off to go travelling around the world to discover new foods and wines? What is your itinerary of 2–3 countries?

New Zealand. Somewhere I've always wanted to visit and home of my friend Theo, winemaker of extraordinary wines at Hermit Ram.

France. I couldn't take a year off and not visit France! Jura for its beauty and uncompromising wines, Burgundy because pinot doesn't get any better and Bordeaux to explore the new and the old.

What is the best advice you've been given that has helped you along the way?

'Go with your heart'. A very good friend I've sadly lost touch with taught me this when I was just 17 and I can't thank her enough—there are lots of times in life when decisions become incredibly difficult to make, I always heed this advice because if I didn't, win or lose, I know I'd regret it later.

Who are the four people you'd dream about having dinner with?

Kenny Dalglish for his incredible talent but also because he's one of the true gentlemen.

A 16th Century Westwell monk to find out about an amazing changing time but also their viticulture and winemaking.

Kurt Vonnegut as his way of seeing the world was just so fresh and innovative.

My wife Galia as she always makes an occasion special and fun.

What was your most memorable food/wine pairing in a restaurant?

Tokaji and custard tart at a Gary Rhodes Restaurant. I could have chosen a lot of things here, first proper Pinot Noir, first glass of Vin Jaune with Comte but the Tokaji and Tart win out as it was probably the first time I realised wine could be something more, something ethereal and uplifting.

Is there something nobody knows about you? Or something people don't realise?

I have a tattoo on the side of my head! When I was young I travelled all around the UK and used to shave my head every few months instead of getting a haircut, I had a tattoo done to remind me of this time but these days it's under hair and hat!

If you were not working in a vineyard, what profession would you like to have learnt?

When I worked in music I spent a lot of time helping others with their creativity but I've realised I enjoy the making process immensely so it would be something that uses those skills—or an archaeologist as I still find the idea of uncovering history fascinating.

You are given (unlimited) funds to acquire another vineyard of your choice? Which one would you buy?

I think Westwell has the *terroirs* to produce really special wines so I'm very happy where I am but I've become fascinated by what's happening in Bordeaux right now and the chance to make red wine from some of the most outstanding grapes in the world would be sorely tempting.

If you could have one superpower, what would it be?

Supersonic flight. Being able to go anywhere in the world without damaging the environment would be so cool!

What is your most unusual food/wine combination that you would recommend?

I don't know if it's really that unusual anymore but as my wife Galia nearly always prefers red wine we've drunk a lot of chilled Cabernet Franc and Gamay with fish and it's become a real favourite, one of the first signs of Summer!

What is the biggest myth about prestigious wines?

I guess price vs pleasure. Drinking good wine with great friends is one of life's best pleasures and that pleasure isn't increased as the price of the wine increases but more by the company.

Do you have a funny anecdote about a vintage that went wrong (or nearly went wrong)?

First vintage at Westwell, attempting to make wine in a very small space a pump was turned on before the tank was opened! The resulting explosion left an outline of my friend Adam on the side of the press as he took the full force of destemmed Pinot Noir... that was a very quick and very funny learning experience.

How do you relax outside of work?

Whilst I work on the North Downs, I live in the South so I spend a lot of time mountain biking with friends and swimming in the sea with my daughters, a perfect day would then finish with a long walk with my wife and dinner in a Brighton restaurant.

What advice would you have for your 21-year-old self?

I've always found that learning from mistakes is invaluable so I probably would just say—'it all works out pretty special in the end!'

What is the grape variety (other than your own) you would have liked to work with?

There's a pretty long list here of grapes that I'd love to be able to play with... all the Juran varieties but especially Trousseau that makes a wonderful light red in the right hands, Cabernet Sauvignon, Nebbiolo, Gamay and Albarino.

Pretty much all because they have so many different sides to them and that endless fascination is what keeps us experimenting and learning

What surprising wine (from a different region) do you have in your wine cellar?

Probably not that surprising but the only wine I really collect is Vin Jaune; most of the wine I buy is ready for drinking but I have tucked away a few bottles of Jean Louis Chave's incredible Hermitage and Vin Jaunes from Bornard, Puffeney, Tissot and Domaine de la Pinte.

Veronique Drouhin-Boss

4TH GENERATION WINEMAKER,
MAISON JOSEPH DROUHIN, BURGUNDY, FRANCE
DOMAINE DROUHIN OREGON, WILLAMETTE VALLEY, USA

You take one year off to go travelling around the world to discover new foods and wines? What is your itinerary of 2–3 countries?

New Zealand, I have never been there and find a lot of their wines to be really exciting. The landscape seems spectacular. I would then go to Lebanon, to discover the food, wines, culture and architecture. Finally, I dream of seeing the cellar of Massandra in Crimée where the wine collection has such an extraordinary story.

What is the best advice you've been given that has helped you along the way?

Never doubt that you deserve your opportunity.

Who are the four people you'd dream about having dinner with?

If it doesn't matter if they are alive or dead:

Mozart. I would suggest he takes better care of his health. We would have many more beautiful pieces of music.

Sean Connery. His favourite white wine was our Clos des Mouches. Big fan of this actor.

Louis de Funès, the French comedian, because I know I would have big laughs, drink delicious wines and eat great food

Louis XIV in Versailles to see the chateau and the garden at the time of its glory. Eating and drinking with His Majesty would fascinate me.

What was your most memorable food/wine pairing in a restaurant?

Musigny 1856, I don't remember what it was paired with. The wine took over the entire space in the room. It was an incredible moment.

Is there something nobody knows about you? Or something people don't realise?

Some people think I live in Oregon since I have made the wine for our estate Domaine Drouhin from day one (1988) but in fact my permanent residence is in Burgundy. I travel back and forth to DDO regularly.

If you were not working in a vineyard, what profession would you like to have learnt?

I would have loved to have been a pianist.

You are given (unlimited) funds to acquire another vineyard of your choice? Which one would you buy?

Without a doubt I would buy my neighbours' vineyards in Vosne Romanée's les Petits Monts. I am lucky to own a parcel of this incredible land, located just above Richebourg. The wine from that site is just stunning, it combines all the beauties of Pinot Noir. Complexity, refinement and elegance.

If you could have one superpower, what would it be?

Bring peace on earth.

What is your most unusual food/wine combination that you would recommend?

Clos des Mouches white with Epoisse (a great cheese

from Burgundy, strong smell, mild taste) or Clos des Mouches red with salmon cook 'à l'unilatérale'.

What is the biggest myth about prestigious wines?

Some think they will age forever. They don't. They have a life and at some point need to be enjoyed.

Do you have a funny anecdote about a vintage that went wrong (or nearly went wrong)?

When something goes wrong with a vintage it is rarely funny but it can be related to very special moments. The most recent example is the frost that occurred in Burgundy on April 6th, 7th and 8th, 2021. Many of us went at night to light candles. It was a great time of teamwork, and it was an extraordinary spectacle.

How do you relax outside of work?

I see friends. Spring to Fall I work in my garden. In Winter, I relax by the fireplace reading, cooking or watching good movies.

What advice would you have for your 21-year-old self?

Travel thru the world as much as you can.

What is the grape variety (other than your own) you would have liked to work with?

Sauvignon Blanc. When well made, I just love it.

What surprising wine (from a different region) do you have in your wine cellar?

I had a bottle of wine made from the Kiwi fruit that was quite good and next I am looking forward to trying a wine made in Japan by a Burgundian friend.

Sandy Moss

FOUNDER, *NYETIMBER*, WEST SUSSEX, UNITED KINGDOM

You take one year off to go travelling around the world to discover new foods and wines? What is your itinerary of 2–3 countries?

Italy and France, where food is more a part of the culture. I would head for the countryside rather than the cities and choose the simple seasonal fare. I think that is where the heart of food lies. I would go to where 'farm to table' isn't a trendy new notion but the way life has always been. And I would go to the seaside for the joys of the bounty of the sea. I like the idea that what you have to choose from to eat at any given time is determined by the bounty of nature.

What is the best advice you've been given that has helped you along the way?

I'm not sure it was advice given to me but I have always felt that to get anywhere you just have to get on with it— whatever IT is. Don't agonize. Don't psychoanalyze. Think things through of course, and then just do it. I've been right far more often than wrong, but a wrong decision can usually be corrected and no decision at all leaves you nowhere.

In terms of winemaking: a friend, a champenois, was taking us through his winery while we discussed the tanks and other equipment we planned for our own winery. He stopped and said with the utmost seriousness that no matter what else, we MUST purchase decanting valves for our tanks; and he was right. They were expensive, but with them I could rack wine off the lees from one tank to the next quicker, cleaner, and with far less loss. They paid for themselves in wine that was not lost in production.

Who are the four people you'd dream about having dinner with?

First would be Queen Elizabeth I because that has always been the first name to come to mind whenever this question came up. A woman in a man's world if ever there was one, and at a time when killing to obtain your goal was not unheard of. And how different history could have been had she not been so strong willed. I would love to understand how she managed the brave front against all of those around her.

Next, would be the Widow Cliquot, another strong woman in a man's world. On the death of her husband, she eschewed her company's other activities and turned her attention to perfecting the technique of riddling. She perfected a method for disgorging the sediment produced during the second fermentation in bottle-fermented wine, allowing for a clean and sparkling result.

I would love to meet Miss Jane Marple, the fictional detective created by Agatha Christie. She was a little old spinster lady with a 'mind like a steel trap.' Wouldn't it be fun to observe her as she unravelled some complex mystery before the cheese course, or just to share a discussion with her, noting her observations. Maybe just a bit might rub off on me.

My fourth guest would be Sister Wendy Beckett, the self-taught art historian and lecturer. In an amazing set of circumstances, she split her life between maintaining a strict code of silence and lecturing, teaching, broadcasting, and writing about art. I find her unique perspective on art to be totally mesmerizing. Listening to her lectures has given me a much deeper appreciation of art.

What was your most memorable food/wine pairing in a restaurant?

We were invited to a party held on the host and hostess's barge moored in the River Thames below London's Albert Bridge. Nyetimber was being served and had been resting on ice in the bathtub. It was a very hot day and the wine was brought up on deck and poured into paper cups, paired with the spicy cuisine of the hostess's native Mauritius. It was a wonderful day and a great party. I have always felt that this was what making wine was all about. If it couldn't stand up to a party of friends—no matter how adverse the conditions—then there was no point.

Is there something nobody knows about you? Or something people don't realize?

At university I studied archaeology. Before moving to England, I had an antiques shop in Chicago specializing in English oak furniture from the 16th and 17th centuries.

If you were not working in a vineyard, what profession would you like to have learnt?

Were it not for the vineyard, I think I would like to have stayed with the antiques. I would have focused on explaining the social and historical context represented by the carving and construction details of each piece. It would be archaeology in another form.

You are given (unlimited) funds to acquire another vineyard of your choice. Which one would you buy?

Given unlimited funds, I would find a site and plant again. There could never be the same satisfaction in acquiring an existing vineyard. I think you have to sweat your own sweat and bleed your own blood and hit your own head against the wall before you earn the right to put your own name on the bottle.

If you could have one superpower, what would it be?

I don't know if it is a 'superpower' but during my winemaking years it would have been super powerful to have had unlimited energy. There was always more to do than there was the energy to do it. Along with that, I'd like to have had more hours in the day.

What is your most unusual food/wine combination that you would recommend?

One of my favourite food and wine pairings is as much a product of association as it is of compatibility. Each year before harvest I would lay in kitchen supplies. One of my best finds was a premade heat-and-serve garlic bread. Almost every night when we came in from the winery, wet, cold and exhausted, I would throw a loaf into the Aga while we peeled off layers of wet, sticky clothes. The combination of the garlic bread and a bottle of Nyetimber was perfect—carbs for comfort and lots of butter to help the wine slide down. The pairing, to this day, is still a favourite even if it is no longer required to have the same healing effect.

What is the biggest myth about prestigious wines?

I think the biggest myth about prestigious wines is that they are necessarily 'better' than other wines. A quality wine earns prestige because of a reputation based on the wine's history, and the palate of wine judges. One would expect any prestigious wine to be well and cleanly made. But beyond that, 'better,' like beauty, is in the eye—and palate—of the beholder.

Do you have a funny anecdote about a vintage that went wrong (or nearly went wrong)?

Thank goodness, no, I have no antidote about a vintage going wrong! Maybe it was that the wine gods smiled or just that our number hadn't come up yet, but no vintage went wrong.

How do you relax outside of work?

I am retired now, living in California, so I no longer require the same down time as those still on the go. After a long day in the winery, I used to do needlepoint because it kept me from falling asleep in my soup! I now walk on the beach, weave baskets, and still do needlepoint.

What advice would you have for your 21-year-old self?

I was a lot older than 21, when we moved continents, disregarded the trends, and committed to planting a vineyard! We had no idea of what would be involved or how long it would take. Frankly, we didn't even know that much about sparkling wines! The stories speak of two crazy Chicagoans who knew how well it would all turn out, but really it's about putting one foot in front of the other, and taking one day at a time. And having lots of warm socks.

What is the grape variety (other than your own) you would have liked to work with?

Rather than working with another variety, I would like to have had the time to make a still pinot noir. It was always the first variety to be harvested each year, and with the entire harvest ahead, focusing on a still red was impossible. We did make a small amount of red in order to make a rose but a real pinot noir would have required much more dedication than I could give it.

What surprising wine (from a different region) do you have in your wine cellar?

Two answers come to mind. My immediate response was a 1993 Tokaji, a Hungarian dessert wine made sweet by botrytis. We bought three or four bottles many years ago and I loved the ones we drank. I loved not only the wine but also the idea of the wild yeast in the cellars where Tokaji is made. When we were moving our personal cellar from Nyetimber, I dropped a bottle, leaving only one. Now I am doing what I tell people NEVER to do; I'm saving it for... I have no idea what I'm saving it for.

The second answer is that our cellar contains quite a collection of English still white wines from the early 1980s. These wines stand as a reminder of those who went before us, and what gave us the courage to go in a different direction—producing sparkling wine from classic varieties.

Anne Malassagne

OWNER, *CHAMPAGNE AR LENOBLE*, CHAMPAGNE, FRANCE

You take one year off to go travelling around the world to discover new foods and wines? What is your itinerary of 2–3 countries?

Italy because I love everything in Italy, wines, food, culture, country; South Africa because their wines are so good and show a new face of this country; New Zealand because I have never been there. It is so far in so many ways but we share the same passion about wines. It is an amazing country I would love to explore once.

What is the best advice you've been given that has helped you along the way?

Never give up and follow your beliefs

Who are the four people you'd dream about having dinner with?

My father who died 13 years ago. He has been my mentor and I would love to show him how much I did to increase the awareness of our family-owned estate

Simone Weil. She had such a fantastic background and she did so much for her country and for women

Leonard de Vinci. He was a genius nobody recognized as a great artist. He had to fight all his life to practice his art.

Charlie Chaplin to have fun

What was your most memorable food/wine pairing in a restaurant?

I love simple pairings. My most memorable pairing is Souffle Suissesse at Le Gavroche and AR Lenoble Grand Cru Blanc de Blancs. Michel Roux is a talented chef and his father Albert Roux was one of my mentors.

Is there something nobody knows about you? Or something people don't realise?

Yes there is something nobody knows about me, and I will not reveal this secret in this letter!

If you were not working in a vineyard, what profession would you like to have learnt?

I wish I would be a doctor like my oldest brother. He gave his life for his patients. Saving lives is a fantastic job.

You are given (unlimited) funds to acquire another vineyard of your choice? Which one would you buy?

I would buy other vines in Champagne, close to the ones I inherited from my parents.

If you could have one superpower, what would it be?

I would save sick children.

What is your most unusual food/wine combination that you would recommend?

I don't eat much red meat but I like it occasionally with a red wine from Château du Moulin à Vent, certainly the best Beaujolais I ever had.

What is the biggest myth about prestigious wines?

I would say: that they are the best wines in the world.

How do you relax outside of work?

I practice sports 3 times a week, mainly floor dance, swimming and running. It helps me relieve stress and keep fit.

What advice would you have for your 21-year-old self?

Follow your path, trust your intuition, work hard and be happy. You live only once.

What is the grape variety (other than your own) you would have liked to work with?

Riesling because I love wines from Alsace.

What surprising wine (from a different region) do you have in your wine cellar?

I love wines from Austria, especially the white ones. Very clean, fresh and straight.

Armand Heitz

OWNER, BURGUNDY, FRANCE

You take one year off to go travelling around the world to discover new foods and wines? What is your itinerary of 2–3 countries?

Only Europe because I don't like planes, I'm very afraid of taking them. With covid it's not easy. It's not very healthy for the earth. And I'm not a big fan of big cities: too many people, too many buildings, too much pollution, not enough nature. I would be very interested to go to places where nature is very present. Sometimes you don't need to go very far to discover new things.

What is the best advice you've been given that has helped you along the way?

Stop doing what people want ! Do what you think is good for you.

Who are the four people you'd dream about having dinner with?

Jacques Tati a French film maker. Playtime is my favourite film ever. He is one of the first to criticise our modern civilisation.

Vaclav Smil. He is maybe one the most influential people covering climate change.

Beethoven or Vivaldi because I'm a fan of classical music.

The last one is a friend of mine Rudy Ricciotti; a French architect who enjoys nature, French knowledge of building.

What was your most memorable food/wine pairing in a restaurant?

Meursault Perrières 1966 on a 18 months Comté cheese in 2007. It was at dinner at a friend's estate.

Is there something nobody knows about you? Or something people don't realise?

I don't like school at all. Going to school is the best way to make human like sheep.

If you were not working in a vineyard, what profession would you like to have learnt?

At the estate, we now make vegetables, honey, meat from cows and sheep, so I'm more of a farmer than a winemaker. I also enjoy sailing. I hope one day I will have time to sail again.

You are given (unlimited) funds to acquire another vineyard of your choice? Which one would you buy?

The only thing which is important for me is to have animals, fields to grow cereals, fruits and vegetables.

If you could have one superpower, what would it be?

To speak with a tree or a plant.

What is your most unusual food/wine combination that you would recommend?

The best way to appreciate a wine is on its own.

What is the biggest myth about prestigious wines?

It is just about money.

Do you have a funny anecdote about a vintage that went wrong (or nearly went wrong)?

2016 and 2019 were difficult vintages in the vineyard, mainly because of frost. When a vintage is hard in the vineyard, it's quite difficult for the winemaker to appreciate the wine. But the wines are showing pretty well today.

How do you relax outside of work?

Sport, tasting with friends, family,

What advice would you have for your 21-year-old self?

Stop doing what other people want! Do what you think is good for you.

What is the grape variety (other than your own) you would have liked to work with?

I don't like the modern vision we have of grape variety. In real nature, the grape variety is always changing and this is how the real nature works. So my favourite grape variety is the grape variety which will appear tomorrow.

What surprising wine (from a different region) do you have in your wine cellar?

Not surprising just different ones from Burgundy, Riesling from Germany.

Berenice Lurton

OWNER, *CHATEAU CLIMENS*, SAUTERNES, FRANCE

You take one year off to go travelling around the world to discover new foods and wines? What is your itinerary of 2-3 countries?

Italy first, as I'm so fond of its landscapes, culture, language and of course food and wines. I especially think that Italy has kept its regional traditions and authenticity in terms of food (more than in France, alas). France: maybe that's my country but there are so many different regions and great vineyards to explore! Then, after staying in Europe, I would go very far to visit New-Zealand, which seems a magnificent country with a real care for the environment, and I don't know much about their wines (food might not be as interesting, but who knows?). Of course, there are so many other countries I would like to explore...

Who are the four people you'd dream about having dinner with?

I would really love to have dinner with François Cheng, a Chinese-French author who has really spoused the French language (he now belongs to L'Académie Française) and made a link between both cultures. I really admire his writing as a poet, novelist, philosopher, and he's a man with an incredible life and most of all a beautiful soul.

What was your most memorable food/wine pairing in a restaurant?

There were so many ones, but I remember particularly having fallen in love with a Sicilian wine in Cefalu, the food was not 'gastronomic' but authentic and made with natural and beautiful products, and the wine had personality: a simple but so enjoyable moment.

Is there something nobody knows about you? Or something people don't realise?

Although I'm a very sincere and direct person, I of course have my secret garden... and won't say more!

If you were not working in the food and wine industry, what profession would you like to have learnt?

I would have loved to be a dancer and choreographer, but I never had the physical qualities required. So, in fact I don't know what I could have done, life has brought me where I am, that's all I know...

What is your most unusual food/wine combination that you would recommend?

Sauternes, and especially my wine, Château Climens, with spicy food: it's more common now, but many people have not discovered this exciting match!

What is the biggest myth about prestigious wines?

That all prestigious and expensive wines are good: some are not at all at the right level, they often lack of personality due to standardization and the degradation of the terroirs with the use of pesticides.

How do you relax outside of work?

Going for walks in the countryside with my dog, having dinner with good friends, taking a nap in the company of my cat, reading, gardening, listening to music, watching films with my son, bathing in summer, dancing, meditating... and travelling when it's possible!

What advice would you have for your 21-year-old self?

Learn to know and cultivate your inner-self, your skills, your deep personality, and believe in yourself, whatever happens! And also: nothing is as important as you think, life is a (strange) game!

What surprising wine do you have in your wine cellar?

Hum, I've got to put it in order to rediscover my gems!

Leanne De Bortoli

OWNER, *DE BORTOLI WINES*, AUSTRALIA

You take one year off to go travelling around the world to discover new foods and wines? What is your itinerary of 2–3 countries?

Italy, France and Portugal. They are old countries that we have visited many times but still draw a lot of inspiration from their food and culture... and of course wine. Portugal is of particular interest because their grape varieties are well suited to a warmer climate like we have in Australia. And the food is pretty good too.

What is the best advice you've been given that has helped you along the way?

Whenever we visit a new country/region, the first thing we do is visit the local bottle shop and buy one or two wines. We ask the proprietor for places they recommend to eat/visit and we usually get the good local intel rather than the touristy spots. We have discovered some amazing restaurants this way.

What was your most memorable food/wine pairing in a restaurant?

Pan-fried John Dory fish with an excellent Chardonnay or Chablis. Always a great combo. But then so is Picpoul with oysters. Also, the chef from our restaurant made some gnocchi with locally picked pine mushrooms (saffron milkcaps) that went smashingly with Gamay.

If you were not working in a vineyard, what profession would you like to have learnt?

An artist

You are given (unlimited) funds to acquire another vineyard of your choice? Which one would you buy?

Domaine Tempier in Bandol in the South of France. I love that area; good honest food, lovely Rosé wines.

If you could have one superpower, what would it be?

To slow down time to have more fun.

What is your most unusual food/wine combination that you would recommend?

We make a Botrytis Semillon dessert wine that most people would pair with dessert but it matches so well with blue cheese. Salty, sweet, smooth, delicious

Do you have a funny anecdote about a vintage that went wrong (or nearly went wrong)?

Every year there are some strange things that happen... or nearly happen but I have promised not to embarrass the people who made those mistakes so their secret is safe with me! Well except for the guy who forgot to apply the brakes on the truck and it ended up in the dam. He thought someone had stolen it because it wasn't where he had parked it. Fortunately no-one was injured.

How do you relax outside of work?

Head to the seaside where there is not a grapevine in sight!

What advice would you have for your 21-year-old self?

Give everything a go. It is okay to make mistakes if you learn from them. Don't get so caught up in the nitty gritty.

And take time out to enjoy yourself.

What is the grape variety (other than your own) you would have liked to work with?

We are in the fortunate position of being able to trial a lot of different varieties here in Australia. We have vineyards in the Yarra Valley, King Valley and Heathcote (in Victoria) and Riverina and Hunter Valley (in NSW). However at the moment we are really enjoying the wines of Sicily, Campania and Santorini—all places with volcanic soils, near the coastline and the wines have a wonderful saltiness about them that goes so well with food, especially seafood.

SOMMELIERS

MIXOLOGISTS

BAR OWNERS

WINE MERCHANTS

Stefan Neumann

MS, DIRECTOR OF WINE, *DINNER BY HESTON BLUMENTHAL*, LONDON, UK

You take one year off to go travelling around the world to discover new cuisines? What is your itinerary of 2–3 countries?

Hong Kong. To master making Dim Sum.

Argentina. To up my BBQ game.

Japan. There is a beauty in simplicity and purity.

What is the best advice you've been given that has helped you along the way?

Listen to your guests and colleagues, it is the easiest thing, all it requires is your attention.

Who are the four people you'd dream about having dinner with?

My grandfather who passed away when I was 14. He never saw my love for wine. I would love to show him.

The late Chester Bennington from the band Linkin Park. He surely has a few good stories to share.

Angelina Jolie. And why? Sometimes it's better not to explain yourself.

Johann Henschke, he would sort out the wine so I can simply enjoy it.

What was your most memorable meal as a customer in another restaurant than your own?

Tickets in Barcelona. Stunning from start to finish. The cuisine, staff, wine, just everything was perfect.

Is there something nobody knows about you? Or something people don't realise?

I am a huge history buff. One of my favourite quotes is: 'Those who do not remember the past are condemned to repeat it'. By George Santayana.

If you were not working in a restaurant, what profession would you like to have learnt?

Something related to wood I reckon. I love the feel and smell of it so working with it and creating something out of it would be wonderful.

You are given (unlimited) funds to acquire a vineyard of your choice? Which one would you buy?

Henschke's Hill of Grace in Eden Valley, South Australia. I'm in love with the purity of these wines; you can never taste something so good and unique.

If you could have one superpower, what would it be?

Fly.

What is your most unusual food/wine combination that you would recommend?

Aged Comte cheese (36months plus) with young Opus One. Magic.

What is the biggest myth about famous restaurants?

Pretentiousness. I love how down to earth so many great/ famous restaurants are.

Do you have a funny anecdote about a meal that went wrong?

Trying to give someone a shower in fish soup must be up there...

How do you relax outside of work?

Cycling, running, rock climbing. Preferably not all at the same time.

If you were to die and come back as a grape, what would it be?

Grüner Veltliner. It's a harmonious aromatic variety with a spicy edge to it. I appreciate balance and harmony in my life (and wine) yet here or there I like to spice it up a bit.

What advice would you have for your 21-year-old self?

Listen more carefully, write all your tasting notes down, don't be afraid to fail.

How would you like to be remembered?

As a guy who enjoyed life.

10 QUICK-FIRE QUESTIONS

Tato Giovannoni

FOUNDER, *FLORERIA ATLANTICO*, BUENOS AIRES, ARGENTINA

ARTIST OR ENGINEER?
ARTIST

STARTER OR DESSERT?
STARTER

APERITIF OR DIGESTIF?
APERITIF

BOOK, TV OR TABLET?
BOOK

SPRING, SUMMER, AUTUMN OR WINTER?
ALL OF THEM

SEASIDE, MOUNTAIN, CITY OR COUNTRYSIDE?
SEASIDE

STILL OR SPARKLING?
STILL

FICTION OR NON-FICTION?
A MIX

MUSIC OR SILENCE?
BOTH

SIGHT, SOUND, SMELL, TASTE OR TOUCH?
SMELL and TASTE

Ava
Mees List

SOMMELIER, *NOMA*, DENMARK

You take one year off to go travelling around the world to discover new foods and wines? What is your itinerary of 2-3 countries?

A full year of travel, wow! I would say China, for the diversity of the cuisine I love so much and to delve deep into the world of tea. Then travel west though Central Asia and finally make my way to Georgia for the wine, the food, and the feast. It sounds like a pretty good lap around the sun to me.

Who are the four people you'd dream about having dinner with?

AJ Liebling, MFK Fisher, Dorothy Parker, then maybe Turgenev, or Zola, or Brillat-Savarin. The food would probably be terrific and the hangover probably terrible.

What was your most memorable food/wine pairing in a restaurant?

Unmarked bottles of cold manzanilla with fried squid in Sanlucar de Barrameda (I don't even know where we were, it looked like some sort of tiny, crowded football canteen and everyone there was at least 50 years older than us).

If you were not working in the food and wine industry, what profession would you like to have learnt?

Teaching, nursing, curating, drawing, driving, there is still so much to learn and so much more time for all of it! Lord knows you can't be in this business forever. I'd like to open a flower shop in my 70s I think.

What is your most unusual food/wine combination that you would recommend?

I would say the most unusual thing I would recommend is that you drink what you feel like with whatever is coming to your table. So if that is a bottle of Rioja with a dozen of oysters, you do! Dinner is about indulgence. Also, I am not here to lecture anyone.

What is the biggest myth about prestigious wines?

Image is nothing, thirst is everything.

How do you relax outside of work?

One day is for turning the tables by going to friends' restaurants, maybe jump in the water, bike around town. The other day is for reading, fresh sheets and phone calls back home.

What advice would you have for your 21-year-old self?

I mean I had a pretty good time when I was 21 (studying, partying, writing, a secret love affair) but what I am continuously advising myself remains the same: be kind to others and yourself, do not judge and also, Mees, please just open up every IRS envelope pronto and deal with it.

What surprising wine do you have in your wine cellar?

Unlike many colleagues in the business, I don't really have very much of a wine cellar (I hoard vintage clothes more than vintage wine) so those 20-odd bottles are pretty much all kind of predictable: single bottles of favourite cuvées made by favourite people. Plus, always a champagne in the fridge and a genever on the shelf.

Pascaline Lepeltier

MS, RACINES, USA

BEST SOMMELIER IN FRANCE 2018, PARTNER AT
RACINES (NYC) AND CHEPIKA (FINGER LAKES)

You take one year off to go travelling around the world to discover new foods and wines? What is your itinerary of 2-3 countries?

Japan. I have never been (even though I learned Japanese for 3 years). It is a culture I am fascinated by, but if I go, I am not sure I will come back...

India. It is more than a country...it is a food universe....

Lebanon. For its incredible syncretism

Who are the four people you'd dream about having dinner with?

Lalou Bize-Leroy. To be able to exchange about wines, and farming, with one of the greatest tasters who changed Burgundy.

Maria Ressa. For her fight for freedom of speech and access to critical information.

Julia Child. She is iconic, and she must have been SO fun!

Ruth Bader Ginsburg. A modern time hero.

What was your most memorable food/wine pairing in a restaurant?

When I was a young sommelier, I tasted stuffed roasted ortolans—which are small birds—with Yquem 1959, a sweet dessert wine. It was magical!

Is there something nobody knows about you? Or something people don't realise?

I am very very shy.

If you were not working in the food and wine industry, what profession would you like to have learnt?

Philosopher.

What is your most unusual food / wine combination that you would recommend?

Sorrel sorbet with VEP Green Chartreuse

What is the biggest myth about prestigious wines?

"The owls are not what they seem"

How do you relax outside of work?

Surf... If I could, I would really like to be able to go surfing everyday...

What advice would you have for your 21-year-old self?

Work only with people who share your world philosophy

What surprising wine do you have in your wine cellar?

I have a LOT of Chenin!!!

Jane Lopes

CO-FOUNDER, *LEGEND IMPORTS*, LOS ANGELES, USA
PREVIOUSLY WINE DIRECTOR, ATTICA, MELBOURNE, AUSTRALIA

You take one year off to go travelling around the world to discover new foods and wines? What is your itinerary of 2–3 countries?

I would start in South Africa: I've never been, and I think there's a lot of great things going on with wine that aren't exported. And it's supposed to be spectacularly beautiful and just a really amazing experience. Then probably head to Europe to visit some places I haven't been to there: Burgundy (I know!), Jerez, Granada, Croatia, and Greece.

Who are the four people you'd dream about having dinner with?

I probably wouldn't necessarily choose wine people! I'm not sure if this is a 'dead or alive' type thing, but I'll stick with people currently living. Let's go with: Trevor Noah, Amy Schumer, Daniela Soto-Innes, and Stacy Abrams. I think that would be a pretty interesting, fun group!

What was your most memorable food/wine pairing in a restaurant?

It wasn't food and wine, but I had a dish of caviar and walnut milk at Studio in Copenhagen, and the combination of those two was absolutely perfect. The nutty sweetness of the walnut milk with the briny saltiness of the caviar worked so well.

Is there something nobody knows about you? Or something people don't realise?

I'm very much an introvert. As much as I love taking care of people in restaurants, hosting friends in my home (in non-covid times!), and spending time with family, I'm recharged by the time I spend alone.

If you were not working in the food and wine industry, what profession would you like to have learnt?

I like to think I would have studied criminology and become an FBI agent, but writer is probably more likely.

What is your most unusual food/wine combination that you would recommend?

A bourbon & Rutherglen muscat old-fashioned with peanut butter M&Ms.

What is the biggest myth about prestigious wines?

Wines get more particular as they get more expensive, which means a smaller fraction of the population will actually like them. It is not a clear upward correlation of expense and general deliciousness.

How do you relax outside of work?

Baths, yoga, cooking, baking, movies, crossword/number puzzles, and cleaning!

What advice would you have for your 21-year-old self?

Probably the same advice I have for my 35-year-old self: go easy on yourself.

What surprising wine do you have in your wine cellar?

My husband and I just opened a 2006 Liatiko from Crete that was excellent!

Sabato Sagaria

MS, FREE AGENT, NEW YORK, USA

You take one year off to go travelling around the world to discover new foods and wines? What is your itinerary of 2–3 countries?

Spain, Italy and France. They are countries I have visited but I feel that I have only scratched the surface. They that are grounded in tradition, yet continue to innovate. Not to mention, I have no doubt I will eat very well.

Is there something nobody knows about you? Or something people don't realise?

I could grow hair if I wanted to.

If you were not working in the food and wine industry, what profession would you like to have learnt?

Professional golfer. I have loved the game since I first picked up a club as a kid. I think it would be important to continue to do something that I am passionate about. Traveling would also afford me the opportunity to explore the world and discover food and wine in a different way than I do now.

What is your most unusual food/wine combination that you would recommend?

Popcorn popped in olive oil with parmesan and fresh herbs and white Burgundy. You'll never be able to eat movie theatre popcorn again.

What is the biggest myth about prestigious wines?

Price=quality

How do you relax outside of work?

Golf, swim, snowboard, cook.

What advice would you have for your 21-year-old self?

Stay the course, kid!

What surprising wine do you have in your wine cellar?

Marylin Merlot. Not sure why it's there, but I've never had the urge to drink it or get rid of it.

Gioele Musco

SOMMELIER, *SKETCH*, LONDON, UK

You take one year off to go travelling around the world to discover new foods and wines? What is your itinerary of 2–3 countries?

Nice question... I will definitely see Greece because it is the new interesting wine country and their product is the new interesting wave in the wine market at the moment; after that I will go in USA and swinging around between the states and try as much as possible from each of them; and last one, seems a little bit crazy, but wines from China will be on the top market soon, so I will be interested to visit it.

Who are the four people you'd dream about having dinner with?

Nicolas Joly, for understanding better biodynamic winemaking.

Richard Geoffroy, for the knowledge about Champagne;

Gianfranco Soldera, has passed away but fortunately I had a chance to dine with him and I would do it again and again.

What was your most memorable food/wine pairing in a restaurant?

I had a lot of wine pairings in my life, but the most amazing one is the most simple, Grana Padano with aceto balsamico di Modena gran selezione, home made salame and a bottle of champagne from Ambonnay winemaker Marie Noelle Ledru... Astonishing.

Is there something nobody knows about you? Or something people don't realise?

Even if is my job I don't like to drink too much, I prefer to open a bottle of fine wine once at week rather than one a day.

If you were not working in the food and wine industry, what profession would you like to have learnt?

Actor ;)

What is your most unusual food/wine combination that you would recommend?

A seabream with a whisky, it was an amazing paring.

What is the biggest myth about prestigious wines?

The more you spend, the better you drink.

How do you relax outside of work?

Reading books, exercise, smoking cigars.

What advice would you have for your 21-year-old self?

Start before and focus more instead of losing time partying.

What surprising wine do you have in your wine cellar?

Barolo Riserva Borgogno 1958

Patrick Pistolesi

MASTER MIXOLOGIST, *DRINK KONG*, ROME, ITALY

You take one year off to go travelling around the world to discover new foods and wines? What is your itinerary of 2–3 countries?

Japan... no need to say why I guess;

India. It's such a vast country with so many traditions I would love to taste all the different dishes;

Last but not least, I would like to tour the wines of California.

Who are the four people you'd dream about having dinner with?

Nicola Tesla; Lou Reed; Bill Murray and Emperor Adriano. The reasons are in the answer I guess!

What was your most memorable food/wine pairing in a restaurant?

Champagne and Mortadella, a nice dry Champagne with a nice Mortadella from Bologna is a perfect pair!

Is there something nobody knows about you? Or something people don't realise?

I'm a very curious guy; also although if I'm a big guy that made most of his career concentrating on hosting, sense of humour and irreverence, I'm a very shy and sensitive man. It's all a cover.

If you were not working in the food and wine industry,
what profession would you like to have learnt?

I don't really know, I would have loved in my youth to be
an actor (I think I'm happier now), be a pilot maybe or a
historian; I love history...

What is your most unusual food/wine combination that you
would recommend?

I would recommend a Dry Martini cocktail with a nice
piece of Parmigiano Reggiano 36 months, incredible pairing; super umami.

What is the biggest myth about prestigious wines?

That they have to be expensive!

How do you relax outside of work?

Walking in nature with my dog, outdoors in general, traveling, going to a pub where I don't know anybody and
listen to the vibe.

What advice would you have for your 21-year-old self?

Respect the bottle, be always true, fight for what you
think/dream and everything will manifest itself!

What surprising wine do you have in your wine cellar?

To tell you the truth, it is this new wine produced by my
best friend Raffaele Rendina called 'Mastodonte', a beautiful 100% Umbrian Grechetto, delicious and unusual.

Matthias Catelin

SOMMELIER, *DOMAINE DE MURTOLI*, CORSICA, FRANCE

You take one year off to go travelling around the world to discover new foods and wines? What is your itinerary of 2–3 countries?

I would like to visit South America like Peru, Chile or Argentina for the landscapes, local food and the places to visit, including my dream: Machu Picchu.

Who are the four people you'd dream about having dinner with?

Pascaline Lepeltier, a very inspiring person in the wine industry.

Madeon. A French DJ and my favourite music artist of all time; he has had a crazy career.

What was your most memorable food/wine pairing in a restaurant?

I had so many good pairings I could not choose one. I prefer to remember the people I share a diner with and the bottle we drunk together.

If you were not working in the food and wine industry, what profession would you like to have learnt?

Nothing else. It really became a passion, a hobby, something I love to do and share with other people.

What is your most unusual food/wine combination that you would recommend?

I love white wine and cheeses; the flavours are closer: Sancerre wine with goat cheeses, Savoie wine with Beaufort Abondance.

What is the biggest myth about prestigious wines?

Their price

How do you relax outside of work?

Recently I wanted to learn more about cigars. Therefore, I studied and smoked some of course. Otherwise I read books, play video games, go out and play sports.

What advice would you have for your 21-year-old self?

In certain circumstances, I could have done with one or two more years at school (wine school). But to be honest, over the past 6 years, I had the chance to work, travel and meet so many people that I would do the same again.

What surprising wine do you have in your wine cellar?

I have a great old vintage (1978) of Barbaresco from Produttori del Barbaresco Riserva Montefico. I love these; they have a lot of character, the flavours age very well because of the grape variety. The history behind the producers is very rich.

Mimi Avery

BRAND AMBASSADOR, *AVERYS*, BRISTOL, UK

You take one year off to go travelling around the world to discover new foods and wines? What is your itinerary of 2-3 countries?

Croatia. We have started selling a fantastic white wine from the Grasvina grape in the last year—it is very exciting. With Hungary next door, I would love to visit the home of Tokaji as we know it.

I suppose India is producing more and more wine—and as I am also interested in Indian food I can probably shoe horn that in as one of the three.

Japan. I've always wanted to go—did not realise they produced much wine until I got on the Koshu band wagon around 2012. Expensive to retail in the UK but some are gorgeous.

Who are the four people you'd dream about having dinner with?

I have been lucky enough to meet and eat with most of my 'heroes' in the wine and food business—from Wolf Blass, who learnt to blend red wine under the tutelage of my grandfather to Brian Turner CBE, Michelin starred Chef. The owners of Petrus and Yalumba are also close family friends.

There are so many to choose from: I have nearly, but at the moment never, met Sam Neill (of Two Paddocks, New Zealand and also an actor). I have good banter with him on social media, and hope that on a future trip to New Zealand we may meet up.

If, however, we are going with those that have left us...

Andre Simon, who was a Champagne afficionado, and set up the International Wine and Food Society.

Then of course my grandfather—he died when I was 7 but I remember serving wines at dinners that he had in his house and picking up stories and smells of wine.

Madame Bollinger, I believe, was a character, similar to my grandmother, who would be a wonderful foil to Andre and Ronald (her great Nephews, who own the Champagne house now, and they are great fun).

The person alive I am most keen to eat with is Roger Jones of the Harrow at Little Bedwyn, now retired Michelin starred chef, but someone that I think would be fascinating to have dinner with.

What was your most memorable food/wine pairing in a restaurant?

We were at Moro, in east London and I had a mouthful of food and reached for the glass—and thought 'wow this match is perfect'—I realised that I was eating a Greek inspired dish, lamb, mint, feta, beetroot and the wine was an Ageorgitico.

Is there something nobody knows about you? Or something people don't realise?

My degree was in Civil Engineering, when I also played Rugby for my polytechnic (even more surprisingly I played Number 3).

Last year I raised a record breaking £150,000 for the Dolphin Society who work to help keep the elderly and disabled in their own homes for as long as possible, also relieving loneliness and isolation for them.

If you were not working in the food and wine industry, what profession would you like to have learnt?

I was in the Territorial Army, Officer Training Corps when

at Poly, and have always wondered what would have happened if I had continued down that line.

What is your most unusual food/wine combination that you would recommend?

I think that it all depends on the occasion—all wine can go with most foods if you are in the right frame of mind.

What is the biggest myth about prestigious wines?

Not sure there are any myths—because beauty is in the eye of the beholder—I suppose the biggest myth is that you 'have' to like them—if you know their story and the wine reaches out to you then it is worth it, but if you buy it just because it is expensive, you are unlikely to appreciate it for what it is.

How do you relax outside of work?

Friends, food and family; dinners out, dinners in—entertaining up to 12 at a dinner is always fun—sharing wines from Dad's cellar. 7 nieces and nephews with 5 god children are fun. I love to travel.

What advice would you have for your 21-year-old self

Be yourself, be confident because you know a lot... by osmosis—do not get imposter syndrome just because you have the name.

What surprising wine do you have in your wine cellar?

More English Sparkling wine than Champagne—the only wines I buy outside of buying from Averys are English bubbles mainly and some still wine.

Geordie D'Anyers Willis

CREATIVE DIRECTOR, *BERRY BROS. & RUDD*, LONDON, UK

You take one year off to go travelling around the world to discover new foods and wines? What is your itinerary of 2–3 countries?

I would love to do a proper road trip of America. I lived in San Francisco for a short time but sadly didn't get much of an opportunity to travel around the rest of the States. Also, it might sound a little boring, but I always love to return to France. There is such a variety of regional cuisine and many more wines to discover.

Who are the four people you'd dream about having dinner with?

As a business we are currently very interested in sustainability and the environment and consequently I would be very interested to have dinner with Sir David Attenborough. I studied English Literature at university as well as detective fiction so I might add in Sir Arthur Conan Doyle who wrote Sherlock Holmes. Then perhaps Tim Peake the astronaut and Billy Connolly the Scottish comedian.

What was your most memorable food/wine pairing in a restaurant?

I can still remember the first time that I ate foie gras with Sauternes. I cannot think of many better pairings!

Is there something nobody knows about you? Or something people don't realise?

I can make a very good martini.

If you were not working in the food and wine industry, what profession would you like to have learnt?

I am fascinated by buildings so perhaps I might have been an architect or a decorator.

What is your most unusual food/wine combination that you would recommend?

I think that one of my favourite 'unusual' food/wine combinations is takeaway fish & chips with Champagne.

What is the biggest myth about prestigious wines?

That you should be scared of it! All wine is made to be drunk and enjoyed. While knowledge can improve your enjoyment you shouldn't take it too seriously.

How do you relax outside of work?

I love to walk/hike. Preferably somewhere abroad with good views.

What advice would you have for your 21-year-old self?

Travel more.

What surprising wine do you have in your wine cellar?

Perhaps a straw wine from South African producer Mullineaux. Delicious!

Thibault Delpech

MD TAILLAN (SHANGAI) AND OWNER,
REVOLUCION COCKTAIL, **BANGKOK, THAILAND**

You take one year off to go travelling around the world to discover new foods and wines? What is your itinerary of 2–3 countries?

Italy because I love the food, the region, the wines but I am not too familiar with them; South Africa for the beauty of the land, the culture and the rugby!

What is the best advice you've been given that has helped you along the way?

Do not drink during office hours.

Who are the four people you'd dream about having dinner with?

Josephine Baker for what she achieved in her impressive career... but she's dead. Gerard Depardieu for his love of wine and food. Mike Horn for the stories.

What was your most memorable food/wine pairing in a restaurant?

Chateau d'Yquem 1986 with a mango pudding in 1998 in Hong-Kong. The day I understood the meaning of dessert wine and the East meets West experience.

Is there something nobody knows about you? Or something people don't realise?

That I took modern jazz lessons while playing rugby when I was young.

What other profession would you like to have learnt?

Wine making (cellar master).

You are given (unlimited) funds to acquire another vineyard of your choice? Which one would you buy

Probably Chateau Leoville Las Cases... one of my favourites.

If you could have one superpower, what would it be?

Change water into wine.

What is your most unusual food/wine combination that you would recommend?

Laab Moo and late harvest Riesling.

What is the biggest myth about prestigious wines?

That their quality is far better than others.

How do you relax outside of work?

I listen to music.

What advice would you have for your 21-year-old self?

Go ahead, travel and do not think too much.

What is the grape variety (other than your own) you would have liked to work with?

Syrah.

What surprising wine (from a different region) do you have in your wine cellar?

Canadian wine Osoyoos Larose.

Michael Sager

FOUNDER, *SAGER & WILDE*, LONDON, UK

You take one year off to go travelling around the world to discover new cuisines? What is your itinerary of 2–3 countries?

I travelled to many, many places already but my list of new places would be: Ethiopia (I love vegan cuisine and want to understand their food better) and the Philippines (I would love to taste and learn more about food from there).

What is the best advice you've been given that has helped you along the way?

Never say no.

Who are the four people you'd dream about having dinner with?

Probably some famous characters either alive or dead.

My grandfather. He died when I was a kid so I never really met him.

Michelle Obama. She is so inspiring!

Jay-Z, apparently he loves wine!

Kermit Lynch. He has inspired our whole generation of sommeliers.

What was your most memorable meal as a customer in another restaurant than your own?

Faviken, in Sweden. The experience is simply unsurpassed.

Is there something nobody knows about you? Or something people don't realise?

I speak 6 languages fluently.

If you were not working in a restaurant, what profession would you like to have learnt?

Teacher.

You are given (unlimited) funds to acquire a vineyard of your choice? Which one would you buy?

I would try and acquire a seriously old parcel of own rooted phylloxera free vines in Tenerife. They have some that are 200 years old.

If you could have one superpower, what would it be?

Being able to travel without transit time or jet lag.

What is your most unusual food/wine combination that you would recommend?

I love pairing mezcal and Champagne, food is optional.

What is the biggest myth about famous restaurants?

That they are good.

Do you have a funny anecdote about a meal that went wrong?

At one of my favourite meals in Celler de Can Roca, at lunch time in 2016, we got stuck at the restaurant because of a dead serious hail storm and weren't able to leave. It was an incredibly memory.

How do you relax outside of work?

Photography.

If you were to die and come back as a grape, what would it be?

Pineau d'Aunis, not recognised and full of potential! My favourite grape!

What advice would you have for your 21-year-old self?

Never say no.

How would you like to be remembered?

As someone who inspired other people to go ahead and open their own business.

Matthieu Riou

FOUNDER, *GRAIN DE SAIL*, FRANCE

First commercial exporter of organic, biodynamic,
and natural French wines by Cargo Sailboat.

You take one year off to go travelling around the world to discover new foods and wines? What is your itinerary of 2-3 countries?

I will probably go first to Germany, as a great lover of white wines I would definitely love to get to know better the impressive variety and typicity of German wines. Then I will head south to Italy, which is for me the second most interesting place in the world for wines and gastronomy (just after France obviously...). I guess I will end this trip by the birthplace of wine, Georgia, which represent nowadays the past and the future of this beloved beverage with a strong focus on skin-contact wines.

Who are the four people you'd dream about having dinner with?

On the historic side, I would love to have a chat with Jeanne Alexandrine Pommery, better known as Madame Pommery, for her huge contribution to what is Champagne now, especially dry Champagne. Thomas Jefferson would also be invited to the dinner as I love to read about his love story with wine and his implication in the development of wines in the US.

On a more modern side, I would be glad to share a dinner with Etienne Davodeau, a French novelist. The last one, and probably the more important, would be Pascaline Lepeltier because she represents everything that I love: passion, a taste for the dirt, ecological conscience, and knowledge.

What was your most memorable food/wine pairing in a restaurant?

I think that it was in Budapest, Hungary, in 2019, during a trip with my girlfriend Margot. My family offered us a dinner in a top restaurant called Caviar & Bull. The Chef made a bull's tortellaci with braised oxtail, brunoise of vegetables, stout enriched beef jus, fresh herbs, and the sommelier paired it with an impressive local Cabernet Sauvignon from a winery called Fekete if I remember well that mostly produces whites. It was an old vintage, a 2003, and it was just perfect. More than the pairing, the moment, and the person whom I was with were perfect as well.

Is there something nobody knows about you? Or something people don't realize?

I learned all my wine knowledge in the field, working in several wine shops during the summer or winter break, tasting by myself, visiting vineyards during my free time. I did not take any class or get any diplomas until last December 2020 when I validated a WSET level 3.

If you were not working in the food and wine industry, what profession would you like to have learnt?

When I was younger, I wanted to be a baker so I guess if I had not become so passionate about wine thanks to my grandfather, I would have been a baker!

What is your most unusual food/wine combination that you would recommend?

100% Pinot Meunier Champagne with an old Parmigiano Reggiano.

What is the biggest myth about prestigious wines?

Probably that they necessarily procure more emotions than less prestigious ones. I'm 27 and have not had the opportunity to taste a lot of prestigious wines (if by that you mean great Burgundies, Bordeaux, Barolo,

Barbaresco and so on) but the ones that I tasted did not gave me much more emotions than less famous ones made by smaller/younger wineries.

How do you relax outside of work?

I'm a big fan of board games, especially strategy ones, and enjoy playing them whenever I have the opportunity.

What advice would you have for your 21-year-old self?

Don't only focus on French wines, start learning about other European and New World ones!

What surprising wine do you have in your wine cellar?

I am deeply involved in organic, biodynamic, and natural wines, often high range ones and drink 99% of this kind but one of my favourite white wines is a Beaujolais Blanc From Domaine de Penlois, not organic at all, pretty inexpensive but so easy, drinkable, and pleasing everybody I know. Whenever I don't want to put any energy looking for a particular wine it's my go-to.

Julie Dupouy

FREELANCE SOMMELIER, DUBLIN, IRELAND

You take one year off to go travelling around the world to discover new foods and wines? What is your itinerary of 2–3 countries?

In Europe, Italy from North to South to discover the local cuisine in each region and get to learn more about the different indigenous grape varieties.

In Asia, Japan. I have been there a couple of times already, but I would love to spend a couple of months there to travel all around the country, get immersed in the culture and I absolutely love the food there. I would want to learn more about their wines and of course spend some time tasting sake and shochu.

In America, Canada. I would especially love to spend some time discovering the Nova Scotia region and its food and wine culture.

Who are the four people you'd dream about having dinner with?

Michele Obama, Malala, Anne-Sophie Pic and Meryl Streep.

What was your most memorable food/wine pairing in a restaurant?

A ravioli of lobster served with a lemongrass and chervil velouté at Gordon Ramsay's restaurant in London which was paired with a German Riesling from Rheinhessen. The intensity of the wine was matching perfectly the intensity of the dish. The citrus, exotic and mineral notes of the Riesling were complementing incredibly well the lemongrass and chervil flavours and then the freshness of the wine was balancing the creaminess of the velouté. It was simply stunning, and I remember giggling at the time because it was that good (a great wine pairing always makes me giggle with happiness.)

If you were not working in the food and wine industry, what profession would you like to have learnt?

I would have loved to either be a 'nose' in the perfume industry or an actress.

What advice would you have for your 21-year-old self?

It is ok to fail, don't be afraid to do so, embrace your failures—this is the only way to be successful one day.

Neil Walker

FOUNDER, *THE ENGLISH VINE*, UK

You take one year off to go travelling around the world to discover new foods and wines? What is your itinerary of 2-3 countries?

I was fortunate enough to actually do this after leaving my last career. My first three locations were California, Fiji and New Zealand. I would not change this and would love to do it again. The highlight was the South Island of New Zealand and the wine in Otago. After drinking Felton Road Bannockburn Pinot Noir, I knew I wanted to work and make wine.

Who are the four people you'd dream about having dinner with?

Winston Churchill. I would like to get his views on the good and bad points in his life. He also liked a drink.

Nelson Mandela. I think he is one of the most interesting human beings that have ever lived. Just to hear about his life and struggle would be great.

Marie Curie. I lived in Poland for 3 years and became very familiar with her work. I would love to hear the struggle she faced first hand and how she never stopped trying to discover.

John F. Kennedy. I think he would be great fun at dinner.

What was your most memorable food/wine pairing in a restaurant?

The most memorable food and wine pairing is more than just the pairing: the surroundings, the day you have been having and the people you are with all factor into it.

Three contenders for me were L'Enclume near Windermere

(18 courses of wine and food), a New Zealand BBQ (Pinot Noir and BBQ food in amazing surroundings) and Nathan Outlaw's restaurant in Port Isaac. Nathan Outlaw's takes it as was on our mini moon, the day was fantastic, the Sommelier was brilliant and the food was stunning. The whole experience was superb.

Is there something nobody knows about you? Or something people don't realise?

I hurt my back badly when I was 10 in a swimming pool accident. There is a spot on my back that if you touch I have an involuntary reaction. Please do not try and find it as it is not that comfortable when people touch it; my wife and son try to find it if they want to annoy me!

If you were not working in the food and wine industry, what profession would you like to have learnt?

I nearly trained as a primary school teacher but went into banking instead. I reckon I would probably go back to train as a primary school teacher.

What is your most unusual food/wine combination that you would recommend?

Fish and chips and sparkling wine. The acidity of the sparkling wines cuts through the grease perfectly.

What is the biggest myth about prestigious wines?

Wine sealed with corks does not necessarily mean it is a better wine than screw caps. Screw caps eliminate many problems that come from corks such as cork taint, oxidation and leakage.

The other big myth I like is that it was not the French who invented sparkling wine; English scientist and physician Christopher Merret invented Sparkling wine in the 17th century when he added sugar to a finished wine to create a secondary fermentation.

How do you relax outside of work?

I actually really enjoy what I do so basically work 7 days a week. I would say running is the one thing I do if I have a problem that I don't know how to fix. Running seems to straighten everything out for me and breaks down the problem.

What advice would you have for your 21-year-old self?

To not be afraid to fail as that is when we learn the most. I would also say to enjoy the lighter things in life more.

What surprising wine do you have in your wine cellar?

I talk to many winemakers around the world and I am very fortunate to exchange wines. Three countries that I am trying at the moment are Georgian, Switzerland and Polish wine. Some are good, some are not so good! Searching for the hidden gems around the World is what I find a lot of fun.

FOOD & DRINKS EXPERTS

EXPERTS

JOURNALISTS

AUTHORS

Jamie
Ritchie

WORLDWIDE HEAD OF WINE, *SOTHEBY'S*, NEW YORK, USA

You take one year off to go travelling around the world to discover new foods and wines? What is your itinerary of 2–3 countries?

If it was just 'food' or just 'wines', my list would be very different (and much more 'new world' centric), but the fact that it is both means that I need to combine and balance both requirements and would select:

France for both its classicism combined with its innovative evolution in attaining the maximum refinement, harmony and balance in using the best ingredients, with minimal intervention, and turning these raw materials into what are some of the most refined flavours of food and wine in the world

Italy for being so creative in re-inventing both food and wine that is a joy to eat and drink every single day, indicative of the roots of its region and the expression of its people. The daily joy and enjoyment of this constant experimentation means that you are very rarely disappointed.

Spain has been at the forefront of the gastronomic and vinous evolution in recent years and what is happening there today is truly exciting on both fronts. This is the place where there is the most dramatic and impactful evolution taking place and the most exciting developments.

This list is all European, it misses all the excitement and intoxication of Asian cuisines, of Japanese precision, purity and excellence, of the brilliance of Latin American flavours and many other of my favourite foods to eat, but it has been selected for the sophistication of the development of both flavours in both food and wine at the most distinctive and refined levels.

Who are the four people you'd dream about having dinner with?

Francis Bacon. He is my favourite artist—a genius in the truest sense, totally unique and loved wine.

Winston Churchill. For being a brilliant satirist with the greatest wit, as a world leader he had a profound effect on the world we live in and his capacity to enjoy wine and spirits.

Jack Ma. For his business philosophy in the modern world, particularly China, and how he sees wine and spirits evolving in the future—I heard him speak in Bordeaux and he was totally inspiring—he also likes wine!

Lady Gaga. For being so talented, focused and original, with the backbone to be herself and say what she believes in—she must like wine. There is a theme here...

What was your most memorable food/wine pairing in a restaurant?

Thousand year old eggs and Krug 1989 and 1990 at Yung Kee in Hong Kong. A thousand year old egg is an acquired taste for a Western palate and I was astonished at how great a pairing it made with two sublimely great vintages of Krug—the richness, flavour and acidity was a perfect match for the powerful flavours of a preserved egg.

Is there something nobody knows about you? Or something people don't realise?

I wanted to be an actor. A failed actor becomes a barrister. I studied law. A failed lawyer becomes an auctioneer. Each time the 'acting' role is diminished, but there is still a sense of occasion and a performance. There is little audience participation with an actor. There is no auction without audience participation. They are different skills, with 'performance' and 'entertainment' being the common factors.

If you were not working in the food and wine industry, what profession would you like to have learnt?

I wanted to be a professional tennis player, but I neither had the talent nor the killer instinct. Next, I wanted to be an actor, as above—I 'sort of' succeeded...

What is the biggest myth about prestigious wines?

While big expectations can bring massive disappointment, we must remember there are no great wines, there are only great bottles.

How do you relax outside of work?

Lots of sport, travel and time eating drinking with friends—and now our children are old enough to join us, which makes it even more fun to mix generations.

What advice would you have for your 21-year-old self?

As a career, pursue only what you enjoy and makes you happy—and never ever be afraid to take risks

What surprising wine do you have in your wine cellar?

None. All wines are welcome—I love the diversity. 'Variety is the spice of life'—William Cowper

Jitse Groen

CEO, *JUSTEAT*, AMSTERDAM, NETHERLANDS

You take one year off to go travelling around the world to discover new foods and wines? What is your itinerary of 2–3 countries?

Italy and South Africa. Italy has a fantastic cuisine, and is a great country to visit. South Africa is phenomenal too, both as a tourist destination and for its food and wine.

Who are the four people you'd dream about having dinner with?

That's an easy question. With my family and friends.

Is there something nobody knows about you? Or something people don't realise?

I think people do not realise sometimes how much founders are focused to improve their business, constantly.

If you were not working in the food and wine industry, what profession would you like to have learnt?

I have always wanted to be an astronaut. I think running Just Eat is probably a little safer though.

How do you relax outside of work?

I am an amateur pilot. It is absolutely impossible to think about work while flying a plane.

What advice would you have for your 21-year-old self?

Work hard.

What surprising wine do you have in your wine cellar?

I have no wine cellar :)

10 QUICK-FIRE QUESTIONS

ARTIST OR ENGINEER?
ENGINEER

STARTER OR DESSERT?
DESSERT

APERITIF OR DIGESTIF?
DIGESTIF

BOOK, TV OR TABLET?
TV

SPRING, SUMMER, AUTUMN OR WINTER?
ALL OF THOSE

SEASIDE, MOUNTAIN, CITY OR COUNTRYSIDE?
SEASIDE AND COUNTRYSIDE

STILL OR SPARKLING?
SPARKLING

FICTION OR NON-FICTION?
FICTION

MUSIC OR SILENCE?
SILENCE

SIGHT, SOUND, SMELL, TASTE OR TOUCH?
SIGHT

Ian Harris

CHIEF EXECUTIVE, *WINE & SPIRIT EDUCATION TRUST*, LONDON, UK

You take one year off to go travelling around the world to discover new foods and wines? What is your itinerary of 2–3 countries?

Hire a camper van to drive round France to the lesser-known regions for 3 months, then drive to Italy and do the same for another 3 months. For the final 6 months, jump on a plane to Brisbane, and hire a camper van to go down the east coast to Sydney, Melbourne and Adelaide with all the wine regions and restaurants in between... and watching cricket.

Who are the four people you'd dream about having dinner with?

If they are people who are still alive, it would be Gareth Edwards (greatest rugby player ever), Jack Nicklaus (greatest golfer ever), Ian Botham (greatest cricketer ever) and Rory Bremner (greatest, funniest impressionist ever). If I could travel back in time, it would be: Winston Churchill, Queen Victoria, Margaret Thatcher and Ernest Shackleton (explorer).

What was your most memorable food/wine pairing in a restaurant?

Wagyu beef and Beaune 1er Cru in Taipei. I was tired after a long journey and nearly took the decision to stay in my hotel. Thankfully I was persuaded!

Is there something nobody knows about you? Or something people don't realise?

I once had a bath with Rod Stewart, and have met (and conversed with) three generations of the British royal family.

If you were not working in the food and wine industry,
what profession would you like to have learnt?

Musician or professional sportsman.

What is your most unusual food/wine combination that you
would recommend?

Chocolate and Beaujolais—love the clash!

What is the biggest myth about prestigious wines?

That they are meant for investors rather than wine lovers—
all wine is made to be drunk, and enjoyed with friends.

How do you relax outside of work?

Sport—playing or watching—and quality time with family
and a bottle of wine or beer... oh, and cheese!

What advice would you have for your 21-year-old self?

You have a great life ahead of you—don't change a thing
(maybe give your first marriage a miss...).

What surprising wine do you have in your wine cellar?

12 half bottles of Chateau d'Yquem 2015 which I will drink
quietly—on my own, in my old age, and with a plate of
cheese.

Matthew Jukes

JOURNALIST AND AUTHOR, UK

WWW.MATTHEWJUKES.COM

You take one year off to go travelling around the world to discover new foods and wines? What is your itinerary of 2-3 countries?

I would visit three countries—one I don't know at all, one I know a little about and one I have not visited for years and would love to revisit!

I have never visited India and from a food, if not wine, point of view, I think this would be a fascinating country to investigate fully. I adore Indian food and my wife travelled around India extensively in her youth and she is keen to introduce me to its wonders.

While I know some parts of Italy well, I could spend a whole year in this country touring every different region simply because the food and wine scene is so diverse and delicious!

Finally, I haven't been to the US for a long while and there would be so much to marvel at in California, Oregon and Washington State from both a food and wine point of view I would also tour the rest of the country to learn more about their fine-dining hero chefs and legendary restaurants.

Who are the four people you'd dream about having dinner with?

It would be great to bring together four individuals with whom I have eaten dinner in the past (and all four have subsequently passed away) in order to bring them together to listen to the amazing discussions around wine and taste which would unfold. All four had a profound effect on me in my wine life and work and yet I don't know if they ever met one another.

They are Henri Jayer (Henri Jayer, Burgundy), Diana Cullen (Cullen Wines, Margaret River, Western Australia), Robert Mondavi (Mondavi Wines, California) and Aldo Conterno (Poderi Aldo Conterno, Barolo, Piemonte, Italy).

Not only would the wines that they brought along to the dinner be truly amazing but also, I think that the conversation would be absolutely incredible. If they could each bring their favourite dishes as well, the food would be as awesome as the wines!

What was your most memorable food/wine pairing in a restaurant?

1982 Clos du Marquis (back then it was the second wine of Château Léoville-Las Cases, 2ème Cru St Julien, Bordeaux and now it is a wine in its own right) among other fine wines with steak au poivre and chips at Chez l'Ami Louis in Paris. I first visited this iconic brasserie in 1990 and the wine list was extensive and extremely good value. I felt as if I was in a dreamlike state from the moment I walked in the door. I was only 23 years old and it was one of the most extraordinary settings, service, food and wine experiences of my life. I saved up for two years to afford the trip with a few like-minded young wine trade colleagues

Is there something nobody knows about you? Or something people don't realise?

I am extremely ordered and tidy, which drives my wife absolutely round the bend. I am not sure I could cope with my workload without being so disciplined, but I realise that it rather prevents me from being able to truly relax! A random fact is that I am pretty sure that nobody loves pencils as much as I do!

If you were not working in the food and wine industry,

what profession would you like to have learnt?

I have always been fascinated with architecture, but I could never have managed to sit tight for so many years to gain this esteemed qualification. I started working at 19 years old and I loved interacting with people and learning on the job from the very first day and this feeling has never left me. Later in life, I have created my own range of drinks, Jukes Cordialities, and it is extremely fulfilling and exciting. Perhaps I could have benefitted from attending a business course and maybe even a manufacturing course much earlier in my life because I have had to learn a very great deal almost overnight. I love being a wine writer, discovering new wines and telling the world, but making stuff from scratch, learning how to market it, sell it and grow a business is absolutely riveting and I have to thank my business partner Jack, my team, and all of my mentors and friends for helping me along this fascinating path.

What is your most unusual food/wine combination that you would recommend?

I am not sure that particularly unusual combinations exist anymore as most pairings must have been attempted by now. Having written wine lists for a vast array of restaurants for nearly three decades I know that this subject is largely misunderstood and also rather more complicated than most people think, but I can assure everyone who reads this that, if you can get it 'right' or even 'close', the flavour of both the wine and the food are lifted to a very different level of appreciation. My biggest challenge was writing the wine list for Amaya (a Michelin-starred Indian restaurant in Belgravia, London) back in 2004 prior to its launch and we achieved universal acclaim overnight for the wine list which was precisely matched to the exquisite cuisine. I loved working on this project and it is fair to say that we changed a lot of peoples' minds around the world about wine-matching with elite Indian food.

What is the biggest myth about prestigious wines?

There are no myths, only reality and the reality is that some prestigious wines live up to their billing and others fall flat. There are a good few very famous wines in the world which I don't enjoy and many others, whose labels are barely known, who excel. I have tasted wines that defy logic—1830 Bollinger—still amazingly alive and refreshing; 1811 Chabanneau Cognac—the most complex flavour I have ever tasted. I poured a glass for Henri Jayer and he said it was the finest flavour he had ever tasted; 1944 Mount Pleasant Pinot Hermitage—made by Maurice O'Shea and a perfect 20/20 in my notes; 1956 Cantina Terlano—the finest, old dry white I have tasted, which put all old white Burgundy in the shade; 1947 Château Cheval Blanc, 1952 La Mission Haut Brion, 1909 Château La Lagune and 1929 Château Latour, among hosts of other old clarets. These are just a handful of venerable wines which have blown my mind, but there are many more young wines that have done the same and they come along with encouraging regularity which is wonderfully life-affirming and it means that while many reminisce about the 'old days', there is plenty more excitement on the horizon!

How do you relax outside of work?

I spend as much time as possible with my wife and children. I have enjoyed two 'goes' at fatherhood, with two daughters aged 21 and 19 and two sons aged 4 and 2. This means that I have two concurrent fields of view which are engaging, entertaining and involving, for different reasons, within my family and I find this enormously lucky and also rewarding. So, given the chance, I try to spend as much time with them all as possible.

What advice would you have for your 21-year-old self?

Nothing—you can't tell a 21-year-old anything. It is important to allow young people to find their way and make their own mistakes. It is far more important to remind them that their parents or their close circle of friends are waiting for their call to help in any way they can and with answers to pretty much anything you can throw at them if needed! With the confidence of a good back-up team, you can then crack on with life, even if you are not treading a well-worn path, and give it the best go you can.

What surprising wine do you have in your wine cellar?

The rarest wine is a wine from my mother-in-law's old property in Portugal which my wife Amelia and I helped to make and other luminaries (mainly highly-skilled Aussie winemakers), came to help with each year. We served magnums at our wedding in 2010 and it was sublime. We have a fast-disappearing collection, and there is a large amount of sentimentality about this wine and we occasionally open a bottle (always blind for guests) and, it is still just about holding up. We like to think that we had a little part to play in pioneering this style of Alentejo blend.

William Drew

DIRECTOR OF CONTENT, *THE WORLD'S 50 BEST RESTAURANTS*, LONDON, UK

You take one year off to go travelling around the world to discover new foods and wines? What is your itinerary of 2–3 countries?

Japan. Because I have yet to visit the country and its gastronomy is renowned as one of the greatest in the world. To have time to explore it and dive deep into its history would be a privilege.

US. Because it encompasses so many cuisines, cultures, ethnicities and historical intersections. There is so much to sample and learn—from Southern cuisine, African-American culinary history and barbecue traditions to some of the greatest fine-dining restaurants and wine producers on earth.

Middle East. Not a country, but a region, again to explore that which I know little about: Levantine cuisine, Arabic traditions, Lebanese food, Israeli food, Persian history. What an educational adventure it could be!

Who are the four people you'd dream about having dinner with?

William Shakespeare. Knew a thing or two about language.

Chrissy Teigen. Smart, funny, beautiful, loves great food.

Bruce Springsteen. What a raconteur (Bob Dylan is my musical idol, but he doesn't chat much, so sorry Bob).

Katherine Drew. My wife, because I'd want to share the excitement, compare notes and because, ultimately, she's my favourite dinner companion.

What was your most memorable food/wine pairing in a restaurant?

For wine pairings, my first visit to El Celler de Can Roca in Girona, Spain. Josep Roca's passion for wine is infectious and the atmosphere at the restaurant among the warmest in the world. As for the food? Simply brilliant.

Is there something nobody knows about you? Or something people don't realise?

If nobody knows it, that's probably for good reason... maybe people don't realise that I'm a journalist by background, and that I bring a journalistic curiosity to what I do.

If you were not working in the food and wine industry, what profession would you like to have learnt?

I'd like to have had the skill to play cricket to a higher standard!

What is your most unusual food/wine combination that you would recommend?

Different Sherries throughout a meal—it's a much more versatile and flexible form of wine than it's often given credit for.

What is the biggest myth about prestigious wines?

I guess that the more expensive it is, the better it is. It's all about enjoyment in the moment, not prestige, price or bragging rights.

How do you relax outside of work?

Playing and watching sport—but also more eating and drinking with friends and family.

What advice would you have for your 21-year-old self?

You don't really know anything yet, so learn, learn, learn—that way greater enjoyment will come.

What surprising wine do you have in your wine cellar?

A £7.99 New Zealand Riesling from Aldi? Though 'cellar' is pushing it.

10 QUICK-FIRE QUESTIONS

ARTIST OR ENGINEER?
LITTLE BIT OF BOTH, not a lot of either

STARTER OR DESSERT?
STARTERS are always the best moments of the meal

APERITIF OR DIGESTIF?
APERITIF, ditto

BOOK, TV OR TABLET?
BOOK, for sure

SPRING, SUMMER, AUTUMN OR WINTER?
SPRING, it's always hopeful

SEASIDE, MOUNTAIN, CITY OR COUNTRYSIDE?
**SEASIDE, closely followed by countryside.
The food's often best by the sea**

STILL OR SPARKLING?
SPARKLING

FICTION OR NON-FICTION?
FICTION

MUSIC OR SILENCE?
BOTH, but not at the same time!

SIGHT, SOUND, SMELL, TASTE OR TOUCH?
**TASTE, given that it incorporates sight
and smell into it, so I get three for one**

Alice Feiring

JOURNALIST AND AUTHOR, USA

You take one year off to go travelling around the world to discover new foods and wines? What is your itinerary of 2–3 countries?

This is difficult for me because this is what I do in real life. But hypothetically, I'd take two months in Japan to finish a story I promised on sake and immerse myself in the burgeoning natural wine scene. I'd have to go in October and November to catch the end of harvest and the beginning of brewing season.

Onto Georgia. I'd spend four months to see if I'd eventually like to move there, more wine. I'd base myself in Tbilisi, but I'd use this as an opportunity to go into regions I've yet to visit like Svaneti and Tusheti.

Then I'd make a hodgepodge of traveling to see old friends and brush up on regions I need to visit or revisit; I'd start in Greece; the wine scene has gone vibrant there and I'm behind.

Marrakesh, Canary Islands, Andalucía, Barcelona, drive into France through the southwest, up to Burgundy, Jura. Fly to Rome; head to Pantelleria (need to see capers in the wild and understand the scene there) and make good on a promise to ferry with a friend to Corsica and Sardinia.

Along the way, I'd help some friends out with harvest, not sure where, possibly back to Burgundy. I really would love to squeeze in a visit to Copenhagen and meet friends in Noma, we were supposed to hit the vegetable season there, but Covid hit, so alas. I think I'm out of time!

What was your most memorable food/wine pairing in a restaurant?

Cappellano 1959 Barolo and Marta's pizza.

Is there something nobody knows about you? Or something people don't realise?

I spent some of the happiest moments of my life as a Morris dancer and musician.

If you were not working in the food and wine industry, what profession would you like to have learnt?

I'm a writer first. Wine is just the vehicle. I might have gone down the playwriting rabbit hole.

What is your most unusual food/wine combination that you would recommend?

Very spicy Indian food with Lambrusco, like Lorenzo Graziano's.

What is the biggest myth about prestigious wines?

The whole notion of a 'prestigious' wine is a myth. If you're buying or drinking wine for prestige or bragging rights, you're missing the point.

How do you relax outside of work?

Dancing, playing my fiddle. Reading. Cooking dinner for friends. Relaxation is not a word I use.

What advice would you have for your 21-year-old self?

Become fluent in at least one other language. Not everyone is on your side so be careful.

What surprising wine do you have in your wine cellar?

Plenty of Georgian and Slovakian and Chilean.

10 QUICK-FIRE QUESTIONS

ARTIST OR ENGINEER?

ARTIST

STARTER OR DESSERT?

STARTER

APERITIF OR DIGESTIF?

APERO

BOOK, TV OR TABLET?

BOOK

SPRING, SUMMER, AUTUMN OR WINTER?

SPRING, AUTUMN, WINTER

SEASIDE, MOUNTAIN, CITY OR COUNTRYSIDE?

CITY

STILL OR SPARKLING?

STILL (BUT REALLY BOTH)

FICTION OR NON-FICTION?

FICTION

MUSIC OR SILENCE?

SILENCE

SIGHT, SOUND, SMELL, TASTE OR TOUCH?

IMPOSSIBLE QUESTION

Charlie Arturaola

WINE CONSULTANT, JUDGE AND ACTOR, URUGUAY

You take one year off to go travelling around the world to discover new foods and wines? What is your itinerary of 2–3 countries?

The Basque Country in Spain and France... because during the pandemic, I realized I need to know more about my family roots and visit as many cities I can to taste new grapes plus learn and discover old cooking recipes

Who are the four people you'd dream about having dinner with?

My two sons Sebastian and Martin with my two grandsons... it has been a while and I miss them a lot! They live in Uruguay

What was your most memorable food/wine pairing in a restaurant?

The most memorable was a halibut fish sautéed with sultanas, capers, parsley, white wine and olive oil... paired with a bottle of Chianti Classico... the Italian owners of the winery could not believe the pairing with a red wine! Neither could the winery broker (sales agent) in Florida... who is now my wife Pandora!!

Is there something nobody knows about you? Or something people don't realise?

I studied and then worked as a sport broadcaster in Uruguay. Then left to go to Spain in my late teens. Later I fell in love with the vineyards.

If you were not working in the food and wine industry, what profession would you like to have learnt?

English teacher or TV producer

What is your most unusual food/wine combination that you would recommend?

A nice NY beef steak with a long glass of Rose champagne—try it! It would be delicious! What a pairing!

What is the biggest myth about prestigious wines?

Find the wines with the grapes that you love with your birth year on the label!

How do you relax outside of work?

Driving and discovering new sites with my wife Pandora around the Normandy coast.

What advice would you have for your 21-year-old self?

Study hotel management then travel the world. Work in Food and Beverage!

What surprising wine do you have in your wine cellar?

A few bottles of 1982 vintage of Bordeaux... the vintage that made me fall in love with the wine business... and here I am 39 years later!

Nina Caplan

JOURNALIST AND AUTHOR, UK

You take one year off to go travelling around the world to discover new foods and wines? What is your itinerary of 2–3 countries?

I'd like to combine a new part of a country I know (like Italy, which has fantastic food and wine that varies greatly from one part of the country to another); and somewhere I don't—maybe Vietnam, which has food I know I love— but I've only tried it in other countries. Also, I believe they even make some wine there now!

Who are the four people you'd dream about having dinner with?

Someone high up in the Roman Empire who loved food and wine—maybe Lucullus, whose hospitality was sumptuous and who famously insisted on eating as well alone as when he had guests ('tonight, Lucullus dines with Lucullus!'). I wrote a book about the Romans and wine, *The Wandering Vine: Wine, The Romans and Me*, but nobody knows now what their wine actually tasted like. He could tell me.

James Busby, who is considered the father of the Australian wine industry—he brought vine cuttings from France and Spain to Australia in the 19th century. He could tell me all about the great European vineyards before they were devastated by the phylloxera louse, later that century, and about Australia just a few years after white settlement.

Barbe-Nicole Clicquot, the widow ('veuve') who revolutionised Champagne in an era when being a woman in charge of a business was a novelty in itself.

And Lulu Peyraud, who I did actually meet, when she was 99. Lulu was the legendary wife of Lucien Peyraud; he made wonderful wines in Bandol, southern France; she cooked incredible food, and inspired the likes of cook-book writer Richard Olney and Californian chef Alice Waters. When I met her, she no longer cooked (she died last year, aged 102) although she still told great stories. I would have loved to have eaten her food.

What was your most memorable food/wine pairing in a restaurant?

Foie gras with sour cherry vinaigrette with Sauternes, the great sweet wine of Bordeaux. An amazing combination of sweetness, fattiness and tanginess, and the idea of a so-called dessert wine with your starter was a lesson in not assuming everything has to be done the same way every time.

Is there something nobody knows about you? Or something people don't realise?

I started my career as a film critic. I'm still not quite sure how I got from there to here...

If you were not working in the food and wine industry, what profession would you like to have learnt?

Maybe a lawyer. I like arguing. But I can't imagine work that didn't include writing.

What is your most unusual food/wine combination that you would recommend?

Probably the foie gras/sour cherry/Sauternes one above. Although you can drink Champagne with almost anything...

What is the biggest myth about prestigious wines?

At the top end, a wine is like a house: it is worth what someone is prepared to pay for it. That isn't to say that a bottle of Domaine de la Romanée-Conti or Henri Jayer wouldn't be the wine experience of a lifetime. But the relationship between the money and the experience is complicated. There are really expensive wines (some Napa Valley Cabernets, for instance) that I don't feel are worth the money—but there are people prepared to pay it, so objectively, they are. And there are some fairly cheap wines, from places like Australia or Tenerife, that I'd pay a lot more for—but I'm glad I don't have to!

How do you relax outside of work?

Eat lovely meals with my husband (who is a great cook) matched with really good wine—so, not a million miles from what I do for work! Also yoga, walks and hanging out with friends.

What advice would you have for your 21-year-old self?

Be nice to everyone, even people who annoy you or who you think aren't doing their job well. Partly because you may need that person one day, and partly because you don't know what is going on with them, and maybe you're accidentally upsetting someone who is already upset for reasons they aren't sharing with you.

What surprising wine do you have in your wine cellar?

I have lots of surprising wines, partly because we have some friends with whom we do 'blind' dinner parties—the guests have to guess the wine (almost nobody ever gets it right, but that's not the point). So whenever I see a wine that would be really hard to guess—a weird grape variety that few people have ever heard of, for instance—I snap it up! So, for example, a red wine called Margelina from Zambartas in Cyprus. It's gorgeous, and it's a field blend— lots of different varieties all planted in the vineyard—and the vines are over 100 years old. Even the winemakers don't know what some of the vines are so there's no way my friends are going to guess that one...

Tim Atkin

JOURNALIST AND AUTHOR, UK

You take one year off to go travelling around the world to discover new foods and wines? What is your itinerary of 2–3 countries?

If it's places I've never been to, then I'd choose Japan, Croatia and Peru, Only one of those (Croatia) makes very good wines, not sure about the food there. But Japan and Peru are two of the great foodie destinations, and I can always drink sake and pisco.

Who are the four people you'd dream about having dinner with?

Oscar Wilde (wit). Johann Sebastian Bach (I hope he'd play the piano for us). Thomas Clarkson (the man who helped to end slavery). George Eliot (my favourite 19th century novelist).

What was your most memorable food/wine pairing in a restaurant?

It was actually a very malty beer and dark chocolate, eaten at elBulli in Spain. It was unexpected, but so were most of the dishes at that place.

Is there something nobody knows about you? Or something people don't realise?

I won a cup for flower arranging when I was seven. I've still got it somewhere.

If you were not working in the food and wine industry, what profession would you like to have learnt?

I initially wanted to go into the film industry. In fact, I had one of those sliding doors moments when I was offered a job as a runner on The Mission. But I'd already accepted a job in France after my degree.

What is your most unusual food/wine combination that you would recommend?

I'm not sure if it's unusual, but I love Vin Jaune from the Jura and wild mushrooms.

What is the biggest myth about prestigious wines?

That they are only made in a small number of places, nearly all of which are in the classic regions of Europe. Prestigious (and great) wines can be made almost anywhere these days.

How do you relax outside of work?

Reading, listening to music, playing golf.

What advice would you have for your 21-year-old self?

This is not a dress rehearsal.

What surprising wine do you have in your wine cellar?

I'm lucky to have a big cellar, so there are all sorts of things down there. Things I like to surprise friends with are Argentinian Semillons, Tenerife reds, old-vine Chenins from South Africa and (a new favourite) Cinsaults from the Itata Valley in Chile.

Henry Jeffreys

JOURNALIST AND AUTHOR, UK

Author of 'Empire of Booze: British History through the
Bottom of a Glass'; also in The Spectator, Guardian, Economist,
Financial Times and BBC Radio 4's The Food Programme

You take one year off to go travelling around the world to discover new foods and wines? What is your itinerary of 2–3 countries?

I met my wife in Sicily and we've been itching to get back to do a proper culinary and wine tour of the island. Sicily is like a country with incredible diversity in climate, cuisine and wine, all on one island.

We're both huge Vietnamese food fans and we've both long wanted to visit south east Asia. Vietnam looks like such a fascinating and beautiful country.

Finally Spain, my favourite country. I really want to spend a week, a month, a year, in sherry country tasting wines, eating food and using my terrible Spanish.

Who are the four people you'd dream about having dinner with?

In truth, the four people I'd like to have dinner with you've never heard of. I'd much rather see old friends than meet famous people. One of them would be my wife. If I did have to pick celebrities I wouldn't want them to be too clever or the conversation would go over my head and then there's the danger of four big personalities competing for attention, which would be a disaster.

What was your most memorable food/wine pairing in a restaurant?

Probably eating tortellitas de camarones, fritters made with tiny shrimp, in Sanlucar de Barrameda with a few glasses of Manzanilla La Gitana. Delicious simple food and unpretentious wine in a gorgeous setting. It's the perfect combination.

Is there something nobody knows about you? Or something people don't realise?

There is, but I can't tell you.

If you were not working in the food and wine industry, what profession would you like to have learnt?

I'd love to have done something with old cars. I'm not very good at fixing things so it would probably involve being a journalist for a classic car magazine.

What is your most unusual food/wine combin ation that you would recommend?

I can't really think of any. I tend to just drink nice wine and cook nice food and don't worry too much about whether they go together.

What is the biggest myth about prestigious wines?

It is that they are more enjoyable than non-prestigious wines. Often the best wine from a producer will be the cheapest one.

How do you relax outside of work?

I love cycling. Not that I get dressed up in lycra or anything, just 20 miles or so on my old racer with a pint at the end. Going to the pub is an important part of my weekend, or was. I'm also keen on cooking. And reading. I read a lot.

What advice would you have for your 21-year-old self?

Listen more, write more, think more about other people; drink less, talk less.

What surprising wine do you have in your wine cellar?

Nothing really unusual I'm afraid. Lots of Rhone and Bordeaux, some Barbaresco. Quite a bit of English sparkling wine but I do live in Kent, so that's not really surprising. I do have some Armenian apricot brandy which tasted delicious in Yerevan but not here.

Georgie Fenn

BLOGGER (WININGAWAYATTHEWEEKEND), UK

You take one year off to go travelling around the world to discover new foods and wines? What is your itinerary of 2–3 countries?

I am desperate to get to Portugal. Their wines are so fascinating and with all the indigenous varieties it's certainly top of my list. Particularly to meet Sandra Tavares from Wine & Soul, I'm a big fan of everything they are producing. Next I think I'd head to Greece to see Nikos Karatzas and see what latest things he's trying, then maybe finish off with a longer flight over to Australia to the Barossa valley where I would love to meet Fraser McKinley, the chap behind Sami-Odi wines.

Who are the four people you'd dream about having dinner with?

Someone actually asked me this recently and I said David Beckham, The Duchess of Cambridge and Guy Ritchie. So random, but I think we'd just all get on really well and there would be some great wine discussions. You know both Guy Ritchie and David Beckham have extraordinary collections and they seem like really kind people! To make it up to four... I'd want them to fit in too so maybe we could get Jeremy Clarkson there too.

What was your most memorable food/wine pairing in a restaurant?

I actually think it is sometimes the simplest pairings that are the most memorable. And there are often a lot more factors than the food and wine. It depends who you're with, what day of the week it is, if you're in gainful employment and can 'splash out' a bit more. One of my favourite moments in a restaurant was in the New Forest, we'd found a really lovely pub and ordered a load of seafood to share. I chose a 1er cru Chablis and it was just sublime. The minerality alongside the creamy garlic of the mussels is something you just have to sit back and enjoy.

Is there something nobody knows about you? Or something people don't realise?

Interesting question. I wish there was but I'm a real over-sharer so I doubt it!

If you were not working in the food and wine industry, what profession would you like to have learnt?

I work in marketing full-time in the fashion industry so perhaps I would actually love to work in wine full time... I just wish that at school, we'd been made more aware of the huge industry that is FMCG, it would have been life changing.

What is your most unusual food/wine combination that you would recommend?

English Sparkling Rondo with curry, out of this world.

What is the biggest myth about prestigious wines?

That you should like them. Just because they're prestigious, it doesn't mean they're for you!

How do you relax outside of work?

In the winter you will find me hunting and in the summer, I like to go wakeboarding on the lake.

What advice would you have for your 21-year-old self?

To be braver. I knew I didn't really want to go to University but I just went anyway. I think I could have spent those three years doing work experience in London and have found wine sooner.

What surprising wine do you have in your wine cellar?

I have a huge Jeroboam of vintage Prosecco, the serious stuff!

Jacopo Mazzeo

DRINKS JOURNALIST AND CONSULTANT, UK

You take one year off to go travelling around the world to discover new foods and wines? What is your itinerary of 2–3 countries?

The first country would be Italy, my homeland. Having grown up there, I probably know a lot more about its food and wine culture than most, yet every time I go back to visit family and friends I realise there's something new to discover. My itinerary? I would simply travel south to north and try not to miss any of its hidden gems.

I would then travel to Georgia. It's overlooked by most travellers, but in fact, over the past few decades, its wine culture has been influencing winemakers all over the globe. Plus for the Georgians, food and wine are interlinked, which is something that I can easily relate to.

Lastly I would visit Argentina. I love its landscapes, its extremes (it's home to the highest vineyards in the world) and its food. To some degree, it's also a very 'Italian' country. Many Italians migrated there between the second half of the 19th and first half of the 20th century. Many of Argentina's wineries are run by families of Italian origins, and even Argentina's flag was created by the son of an Italian!

Who are the four people you'd dream about having dinner with?

Pellegrino Artusi. He wrote the first cookbook of Italian recipes (in the modern sense of the term) back in the 1890s and people still follow his recipes, myself included.

I would ask him why Carbonara isn't there and solve one of the world's greatest mysteries.

Sigmund Freud. I wish I could tell him how his work helped me develop a critical and analytic mindset.

Angela Merkel. I'd ask her advice on leadership skills and know what she thinks of my cooking and wine choices.

My parents. Because of Covid-19 I haven't seen them in a very long time, and I really can't wait to see them again.

What was your most memorable food/wine pairing in a restaurant?

Pheasant and a light and subtle Grenache with just a few years of age. When it's light, juicy, delicately acidic and a bit earthy, Grenache is divine if paired to game bird.

Is there something nobody knows about you? Or something people don't realise?

I rarely get angry and I'm usually very calm, but often people tell me that at first sight I look intimidating.

If you were not working in the food and wine industry, what profession would you like to have learnt?

Too many to list, but luthier is definitely up there

What is your most unusual food/wine combination that you would recommend?

Pea soup and a delicate Viognier. We always talk about pairing mains, but when you work as a sommelier you realise you need to develop some solid matches for all courses.

What is the biggest myth about prestigious wines?

This one is easy. That they aren't necessarily better than much cheaper wine (within limits).

How do you relax outside of work?

I cook and spend time with my daughter. Often combining the two things.

What advice would you have for your 21-year-old self?

Enjoy your home country and your family, you're going to miss them. Other than that, go ahead with what you're planning to do even though you might face some tough challenges along the way.

What surprising wine do you have in your wine cellar?

Progetto 1, Leone Conti Romagna Albana DOCG Secco. It's a stunning, long-lived dry white made with late-harvest Albana grapes not far from where my parents live. It's one of Italy's greatest whites, and yet few know it beyond the borders.

Simon Woolf

JOURNALIST AND AUTHOR, NETHERLANDS

You take one year off to go travelling around the world to discover new foods and wines? What is your itinerary of 2-3 countries?

New Zealand, because it's part of a whole continent I've never visited—and has some relatively cool climates that I think I'd enjoy.

Japan, and specifically the Hokkaido region because I have tasted amazing things but never visited those vineyards. And the food culture is mind-blowing.

Spain, because of all the great European wine countries, it's one that I know scandalously badly (especially the south which I have never explored). And I know it is filled with great wine, mountainous landscapes and of course tasty titbits along the way.

Who are the four people you'd dream about having dinner with?

That's a challenging question, because there are many people I'd like to meet—but I have no idea whether they appreciate good food and wine or whether they are as sparkling at table as they appear to be in their public personas.

For example, I doubt that most actors or actresses make for fun dinner guests—too busy watching their figures and worrying about their diets.

However, if there is one person who ticks all those boxes

and more, it would be the late Anthony Bourdain. I bet he was fun.

What was your most memorable food/wine pairing in a restaurant?

It wasn't in a restaurant, but I think it's worth mentioning: drinking Nino Barraco's fresh, saline Vignammare together with fresh sea-urchins that he pulled out of a plastic bucket and sliced for us on the spot. We were standing in the vineyards (West Sicily, not too far from Palermo) that had produced the wine, about 50 metres away from the Mediterranean sea. Nino had caught the sea-urchins about an hour before we ate them.

Is there something nobody knows about you? Or something people don't realise?

Although I'm a wine critic/writer, I'm rubbish at describing wines. It really stresses me out! I'd much rather tell you the story of the winemaker, or an experience that made me love the wines (see above).

If you were not working in the food and wine industry, what profession would you like to have learnt?

I have worked in many other professions (IT consultant, interior decorator, sound engineer and others), but would have liked to work in TV or film (on the technical side of things, perhaps as a video editor). I enjoy taking raw material and turning it into a finished work of art.

What is your most unusual food/wine combination that you would recommend?

I was amazed the first time I had raw oysters with quite a tannic, bone-dry orange wine. A perfect match of briny, umami goodness.

What is the biggest myth about prestigious wines?

That they are somehow the best tasting or most amazing

wines of their type. Prestige is really just about the label, so just as with designer handbags or clothes, your money is spent on brand marketing rather than the actual contents of the bottle.

For me there is a sweet-spot in wine, and that is honestly made, artisanal wines from small producers that retail around the £20–£30 level.

How do you relax outside of work?

Cooking is my standard end-of-day relaxation activity. Eating and drinking with friends in general. Yoga helps me de-stress in the mornings, and helps balance the effects of the aforementioned eating and drinking! Before life here in Amsterdam went into lockdown, playing squash was another great release.

What advice would you have for your 21-year-old self?

Be more persistent and ambitious. Waste less time, sleep a bit more!

What surprising wine do you have in your wine cellar?

I have all kinds of treasure! As someone who writes almost exclusively about natural wines and unusual wine countries, people might be surprised to learn that I have a bit of classic Bordeaux and some vintage port stuffed away in a dark corner.

10 QUICK-FIRE QUESTIONS

Jancis Robinson

JOURNALIST AND AUTHOR, UK

FT wine correspondent and author (Oxford companion to wine, world atlas of wine and wine grapes)

JANCISROBINSON.COM

ARTIST OR ENGINEER?
ARTIST

STARTER OR DESSERT?
DESSERT (I'm from the north: Cumbria)

APERITIF OR DIGESTIF?
APERITIF. I've usually had enough to drink by the time I get to the end of the main course

BOOK, TV OR TABLET?
BOOK EVERY TIME!

SPRING, SUMMER, AUTUMN OR WINTER?
SUMMER. Good question. Summer's a bit brash. Autumn is beautiful but melancholy. I love summer!

SEASIDE, MOUNTAIN, CITY OR COUNTRYSIDE?
MIX OF THE LAST TWO, PLEASE. I'm a Taurus so no great friend of water

STILL OR SPARKLING?
SPARKLING

FICTION OR NON-FICTION?
FICTION (plus the odd biography and travel book)

MUSIC OR SILENCE?
MUSIC

SIGHT, SOUND, SMELL, TASTE OR TOUCH?
SMELL! (and please keep that virus well away from me)

Alfred's Recipe

Duck Breast Seasoned with Homemade Sea Salt, Pea Puree and Caramelised Carrots

INGREDIENTS

Duck breasts

Knob of butter and salt and pepper for seasoning

500 g of frozen peas

Lemon juice

500 g carrots, peeled and cut in half lengthways

50 g butter and 1 tbsp olive oil

Thyme

1 tbsp soft brown sugar

1 tbsp balsamic vinegar

1 litre of sea water
(collected in clean milk bottles
from the beach in Whitstable)

RECIPE

CARAMELISED CARROTS

- Blanch carrots in a pan of boiling salted water for 3 minutes, drain well, then pat dry. In a large pan, melt the butter and oil, then fry the carrots and thyme over a low heat for 30 minutes until golden.

- Stir in the sugar and bubble for a few minutes.

- Add the vinegar, then continue to cook until syrupy, about 5 minutes.

DUCK BREAST

- Score the duck breasts with a criss-cross pattern through the skin. Season well, then set aside to bring the meat to room temperature.

- Put the breasts skin-side down in a cold frying pan and slowly heat the pan. This will melt the fat and help the skin to crisp up without burning.

- Fry the breasts, letting the fat melt out and the skin crisp up. Keep frying until the skin is crisp and brown and you've melted out as much of the visible white fat as possible (10–15 minutes).

- Pour the excess fat into a ceramic or glass dish

- Turn the breasts, add the butter and swirl the pan, then cook until the meat is browned all over (the meat should feel soft but spring back slightly when pressed); 5–6 minutes for a rosy pink flesh or 10–12 minutes if you'd like it well cooked.

Alfred's Recipe

- Using a meat thermometer, it should read 54°C for rare, 61°C for medium and 65°C for medium/well done.

- Rest the duck breast for 10 minutes before slicing to serve.

PEA PUREE

- Bring a large pan of salted water to the boil, blanch the peas for 3 minutes

- Add the peas to a blender along with a little water and milk. Blitz the peas, adding more liquid in small additions as needed. Blend for 2–3 minutes, until it becomes a smooth purée

- Season with salt and a squeeze of fresh lemon juice

HOMEMADE SEA SALT

- Pour the seawater into a large pan through a dishcloth and a sieve to remove any leftover sand

- Bring the seawater to boil and stir occasionally

- Once most of the water has evaporated (only 1 or 2 cm deep left), reduce the heat to a minimum

- When it's like wet sand (thick but still pourable), pick up a few spoonfuls of salt and place it on a baking tray in the oven on the lowest heat (150–170°C) to speed up evaporation.

- After a few minutes, your salt crystals are ready